# RAND

# Public Expenditures in the United States: 1952–1993

*John E. Dawson, Peter J. E. Stan*

# PREFACE

The way public expenditures are presented in the federal budget has become an important policy issue, as the Fiscal Year 1992 through 1995 budget submissions illustrate. All of the proposed alternatives focus on the federal sector, however, and none presents the national budget in the context of the national economy.

This analysis offers new, alternative ways of viewing federal, state, and local government expenditures. In doing so, it focuses attention on the major categories of expenditures that will shape the agenda for policy into the next century and illustrates forms of presentation for public expenditures that would benefit citizens and government decisionmakers alike. The information cutoff date for this document is September 1994.

The results should be useful to economic and budgetary policymakers at all levels of government. In addition, members of the public interested in these areas of policy and in the history, relative magnitudes, and control of various categories of government expenditure should also find the results interesting.

Forthcoming reports in this series by the same authors are

- *Public Receipts in the United States: 1952–1993*; and
- *Public Budgets in the United States: 1952–1993.*

This work has been supported by RAND using its own funds.

# CONTENTS

# FIGURES

# TABLES

# SUMMARY

## POLICY CONTEXT

The way public expenditures are represented in the federal budget has become an important policy issue, as recent budget submissions illustrate. However, all of the proposed alternatives focus only on the federal sector; none presents a national budget in the context of the national economy.

The goals of the analysis presented in this report are

- To offer new, alternative ways of viewing federal, state, and local government expenditures;

- To focus attention on the major categories of public expenditures that will shape the agenda for policy into the next century; and

- To illustrate forms of presentation for public expenditures that would benefit citizens and government decisionmakers alike.

To accomplish these goals, we develop four complementary schemes for classifying data on public expenditures from the U.S. National Income and Product Accounts according to the expenditure's *function* (e.g., defense, education); the *fund* that pays for the expenditure (social insurance or "regular budget"); the *jurisdiction* that undertakes the expenditure (federal or state and local government); and the *economic type* of the expenditure (e.g., purchases, transfers). We use these classification schemes to discuss trends in public expenditures relative to growth in the U.S. economy over the past 41 years, focusing on the largest and most dynamic components of these expenditures.

## MAJOR FINDINGS

Between 1952 and 1993, expenditures by all levels of government increased from 26.3 to 33.1 percent of gross domestic product (GDP). This 6.8-percentage-point increase is the net result of a striking 9.2-point decline in expenditures for defense and veterans' compensation combined with a 16.0-point increase in other categories of expenditure.

Our four classification schemes provide complementary views of these expenditure movements.

**From the perspective of the expenditure's function.** Five categories account for most of the increase in expenditures: *Social Security, medical care, education, welfare,* and *police and corrections* have increased from 3.7 percent of GDP to 16.7 percent, thus generating 13 percentage points of the 16.0-point increase in expenditures.

At least to a first order, a small number of factors account for these increases. The successive cohorts of the post–World War II baby boom largely shaped expenditures for public primary and secondary education after 1952, and these expenditures, in turn, dominated education expenditures as a whole. Likewise, subsequent encounters of these cohorts with the law enforcement and criminal justice systems, and especially policy decisions leading to tougher sentencing, drove police and corrections expenditures.

Meanwhile, at the other end of the age distribution, the pool of persons eligible for Social Security benefits increased rapidly over the period, as did the magnitude of these benefits. Medicare expenditures increased partly because of the larger proportion of elderly in the population, but the more important factor in their increase has been the increasing costs of medical care delivery, which some analysts have attributed to enhancements in medical technology. State and local medical expenditures, including federal Medicaid grants, have likewise increased as medical costs have risen. Although these trends have not resulted primarily because of the increased proportion of the elderly in the U.S. population, as the baby-boom cohorts age, the increased proportion of the elderly will play a more prominent role in shaping these expenditures.

**From the perspective of the fund that pays for the expenditures.** *Social insurance expenditures* have increased from 1.5 to 6.7 percent of GDP, accounting for nearly 5.3 percentage points of the net 6.8-point increase in expenditures. Social insurance is that category of expenditures in which the government manages payments by citizens, who expect to receive income based on these payments at some later point in life. The income returned is subject to the political fortunes of the program and may be greater or less than payments actually made, however. Social Security and Medicare account for most of the increase in social insurance expenditures. In contrast, *regular budget expenditures* grew by only 2.4 points, from 25.3 to 27.7 percent of GDP, with net interest payments accounting for the lion's share of the growth.[1]

**From the perspective of the jurisdiction that undertakes the expenditure.** Federal public expenditures have risen by less than 1 percentage point of GDP since 1952, while federal grants, which are intergovernmental transfers of resources, have grown more than 2 percentage points. At the same time, state and local expenditures have risen by more than 6 percentage points, from 6.9 to 13.0 of GDP, and now make up more than one-third of total public expenditures and one-half of domestic expenditures.

The dramatic growth of state and local expenditures and the fact that federal grants link expenditures across jurisdictions both highlight the

---

[1]Interfund transactions, which increased by 0.9 percentage point of GDP over the period, have been deducted from the totals.

need to include all levels of government in an expenditure classification scheme.

**From the perspective of the economic type of the expenditure.** Purchases of goods and services made up 18 to 20 percent of GDP over most of the period. All of the relative growth in public expenditures has occurred in the form of redistributions of income through transfer and interest payments, mainly to the elderly, the poor, and creditors. Transfer payments alone grew by 10 percentage points of GDP.

We can integrate these views to gain a composite perspective on broad trends in public expenditures over the past 41 years. Growth in public expenditures has occurred in

- Federal social insurance expenditures, mainly Social Security and the Hospital Insurance portion of Medicare;
- State and local regular budget purchases and transfer payments, especially education, health (including federal Medicaid grants), welfare, and police and corrections; and
- Federal regular budget interest payments.

## POLICY IMPLICATIONS

Since the late 1960s, federal budgetary practice has attempted to focus attention on a one-dimensional, functional view of federal expenditures in the "unified" budget. In recent years, the shortcomings of this approach have been increasingly recognized, and the principle of viewing expenditures in more than one way has again achieved prominence. To date, however, efforts to devise alternative ways of presenting expenditures have focused on federal expenditures alone, ignoring the critical need to place these expenditures within the context of the total public sector and the total economy.

Classifications of expenditures help shape the debate about the government's role in the economy. The policy issues surrounding public expenditures would be greatly clarified by supplementary federal budgetary presentations that

- Separate federal social insurance and regular budget expenditures, focusing on their very different dynamics;
- Emphasize classification of expenditures by economic type and highlight the different roles of the various types in the economy;
- Include a treatment of aggregate state and local expenditures, focusing on their interdependence with federal expenditures through federal grants;
- Recognize that federal grants-in-aid to state and local governments are "fungible" with other state and local funds; and

- Facilitate decisions on the character of federal expenditures by placing them in the context of total public expenditures.

At a more fundamental level, we suggest that the current federal budgetary presentation is flawed at its base. In particular, it does not address the ongoing need for forms of presentation that enhance understanding of public expenditures and facilitate decisions that shape them. Moreover, alternative budgetary presentations—including those suggested above—are not likely to result in significant progress. It is time to revisit the basis of how the federal budget is presented and to do so with attention to the fundamentals of budgetary communication and taxonomy.

# ACKNOWLEDGMENTS

The authors thank Steve Drezner and Jim Thomson of RAND for encouraging and supporting this research. David T. Dobbs of the Bureau of Economic Analysis, U.S. Department of Commerce, provided technical assistance on the National Income and Product Accounts, for which we are grateful. Mary E. Vaiana of RAND materially improved the exposition throughout the document. We are indebted to Janet DeLand of RAND for her intelligent editing and skillful page layout.

We likewise thank Don Rice, formerly of RAND, and Jack Borsting, former Comptroller in the Office of the Secretary of Defense, who supported and encouraged several precursors of this work. Peter Ivory provided research assistance to the first author during these earlier efforts.

Last, but by no means least, we thank our RAND colleagues, Edward G. Keating and Charles Wolf, Jr., for their penetrating technical reviews of earlier drafts of this document. The latter, in particular, was severe and painstaking, yet thoroughly constructive.

None of these kind individuals is responsible for any errors of fact or interpretation that may remain; these are the sole responsibility of the authors.

## ACRONYMS AND ABBREVIATIONS

| | |
|---|---|
| AFDC | Aid to Families with Dependent Children |
| BEA | Bureau of Economic Analysis, U.S. Department of Commerce |
| COA | Conditions of aid |
| DO | Direct order |
| DoD | U.S. Department of Defense |
| Fed | U.S. Federal Reserve |
| FY | Fiscal year |
| GDP | Gross domestic product |
| HI | Hospital Insurance (Medicare Part A) |
| ISSSW | Income Support, Social Security, and Welfare |
| K–12 | Kindergarten through grade 12 |
| NIPA | National Income and Product Accounts |
| OASDI | Old-Age, Survivors', and Disability Insurance (Trust Fund) |
| OASI | Old-Age and Survivors' Insurance (Trust Fund) |
| OMB | Office of Management and Budget, Executive Office of the President |
| OSD | Office of the Secretary of Defense |
| RDT&E | Research, development, test, and evaluation |
| SGE | Surpluses of government enterprises |
| SI | Social insurance |
| S/L | State and local |
| SMI | Supplemental Medical Insurance (Medicare Part B) |

NOTE:  1.  All years referred to in this report are calendar years, unless otherwise noted.

2.  Detail in tables may not sum due to rounding.

# 1. INTRODUCTION

> *. . . budgeting is a device whereby the same phenomena and the same ideas are progressively translated into differing levels of meaning.*
>
> — Frederick C. Mosher (1954)

Total public expenditures are the sum of federal, state, and local government expenditures that involve payments to nongovernment sectors of the economy. As such, these expenditures provide a means for examining a significant portion of government's role in the economy. The identification, definition, classification, and presentation of public expenditures are basic elements in how decisions about these expenditures are made, as well as part of the content of the decisions themselves.

*Classifications of expenditures help shape the debate about the government's role in the economy.*

The way public expenditures are represented in the federal budget has become an important policy issue, as recent budget submissions illustrate.[1] However, all of the alternatives currently proposed discuss only the federal sector; none attempts to view federal expenditures in the context of a national budget of the public sector intertwined with the entire national economy. This broad context is the focus of our work.

*Current classification schemes do not present a national budget in the context of the national economy.*

The goals of this analysis are

*Goals and tools of the analysis.*

- To offer new, alternative ways of viewing federal, state, and local government expenditures;

- To focus attention on the major categories of public expenditures that will shape the agenda for policy into the next century; and

- To illustrate forms of presentation for public expenditures that would benefit citizens and government decisionmakers alike.

To accomplish these goals,

- We develop several complementary classification schemes, or perspectives, to aid the understanding and analysis of public expenditures; and

- We use these tools to discuss trends in public expenditures relative to growth in the U.S. economy over the past 41 years, focusing on the largest and most dynamic components of these expenditures.

In the remainder of this section, we explain why new ways of viewing public expenditures are needed and describe how we have addressed

---

[1]See OMB (1992: Part Three), OMB (1993: Appendix One), and OMB (1994a: Secs. 2 and 3).

these needs.  We then describe the more important features of our methods.

## THE HISTORICAL CONTEXT OF EXPENDITURE CLASSIFICATION

*The policy concerns motivating our expenditure classifications have deep historical roots.*

Concern with classifying expenditures is hardly new.  Indeed, our classification proposals can be traced to the early years of the Republic, with subsequent enhancements through the 1940s.  To emphasize the long-standing character of these policy concerns, it is worth tracing the broad outlines of this evolution.

*Alexander Hamilton saw well-identified expenditures as the basis for decision-making and expenditure control.*

**Laying the foundations.**  The original architect of expenditure classification for the U.S. government was Alexander Hamilton, the first Secretary of the Treasury.  Well aware of the financial weaknesses inherent in the Articles of Confederation, he welcomed the strength of the Constitution and its key financial provision:

> No money shall be drawn from the Treasury, but in consequence of appropriations made by law; and a regular statement and account of receipts and expenditures of all public money shall be published from time to time (U.S. Constitution, Article 1, Section 9, Clause 7).

Hamilton explained the meaning of this clause in this way:

> The design of the Constitution in this provision was, as I conceive, to secure these important ends—that the *purpose*, the *limit*, and the *fund* of every expenditure should be ascertained by a previous law.  The public security is complete in this particular, if no money can be expended, but for an *object*, to an *extent*, and *out of a fund*, which the laws have prescribed.[2]

**The contributions of Dawes and Smith.**  Little progress was made beyond Hamilton's insights for well over a century.  But with the landmark changes accompanying the new executive budget in 1921, Charles Dawes, the first budget director, renewed the call for well-designed multiple classifications of budgetary information as the basis for government decisionmaking and expenditure control (Dawes, 1921: XLVIII–LII).

*Harold Smith called for a national budget that included state and local budgets.*

Attention to this issue again wavered until Harold Smith's term as budget director from 1939 to 1945.  Beyond his accomplishments in financing U.S. participation in World War II, Smith envisioned two major themes for postwar budgets that closely resemble the themes in this report:

- Consideration of state and local budgets with the federal budget as parts of a national budget, as well as a role for state and local fiscal policy in setting national fiscal policy; and

---

[2]Quoted in Powell (1939:133).  Emphasis is in the original.

- Use of the fledgling national income accounts as an economic framework for national budgetary and fiscal policy (Smith, 1946:114–128, 167–179).

Although great progress in federal budgeting occurred in the immediate postwar years, it concentrated on improvements in microbudgetary estimation and decision processes. Smith's vision of developing macrobudgetary presentations was not pursued.

**The unified budget.** The next opportunity for considering major changes in budgetary perspectives occurred in the mid-1960s. It arose because three different classification schemes for the federal budget existed and gave rise to three different federal deficits.

The President's Commission on Budgetary Concepts (1967) had the chance to structure budgetary levels of meaning that would enhance public discussion and improve government budgetary decisionmaking. Instead, the commission settled on a narrower task and responded to the challenge of the three competing classifications by forging a new method of classification—the "unified budget." This budget was adopted by the Executive immediately in 1968 and by the Congress in its budgetary reform of 1974.

Our research suggests that the advantages of simplicity provided by the unified budget are not worth the accompanying obfuscation of key elements of public expenditures. Moreover, despite its name, the federal budget has had severe problems in remaining unified, with designation of "off-budget" entities beginning in 1971 and the departure of Social Security trust funds in the 1980s.[3] Other aggregate presentations have come into vogue, while attention to the unified budget has declined.

*The "unified budget," adopted in 1968, obscured key elements in the structure of public expenditures.*

**Renewed interest in budgetary classification.** Recent recognition of the unified budget's shortcomings has stimulated renewed interest in the fundamentals of budgetary classification. Attention has refocused on alternative structures for the budget and on restoration of the principle that "receipts and spending should be viewed in more than one way" (OMB, 1993:487). Among these alternatives are a variety of capital budgets, "generational accounting," the funding categories used prior to

---

[3]The term "off-budget" has been used with various meanings since 1971. However, it has primarily designated various federal accounts that are not included in calculating the federal budget deficit—either the "unified" deficit or some other deficit or budgetary constraint of executive or legislative interest. (For the current definition of the term, see the Glossary of Budgetary Terms in OMB (1994a).)

It should be noted that the concept of off-budget expenditures is not relevant to this analysis, since the analysis seeks to be comprehensive by examining all expenditures in all jurisdictions, whether off-budget or not, insofar as they are included in the product and income flows of the economy.

4

the unified budget, and proposals for federal use of typical state budgeting methods.[4]

The thrust of this report is to expand the domain in which public expenditures are discussed to include all governments serving the citizen within the total economy. As such, this presentation is not "the" best new budgetary presentation. Neither does it compete with any of the alternative presentations of federal or state and local expenditures mentioned above, which may also be useful for enriching our understanding. Rather, this report aims to fill a void in the set of proposed presentations by offering alternative means of viewing total public sector expenditures. It thus seeks to be broadly complementary to these alternative budgetary presentations.

## A SET OF NEW EXPENDITURE CLASSIFICATIONS

*Our four expenditure classifications reaggregate categories from the National Income and Product Accounts to highlight the largest and most dynamic components of total public expenditures.*

Consistent with our interest in examining public expenditures within the context of the entire economy, we use four expenditure classifications or perspectives that derive directly from the National Income and Product Accounts (NIPA), produced by the Bureau of Economic Analysis (BEA) in the U.S. Department of Commerce. However, our methods reveal levels of meaning for expenditures beyond those found directly in the NIPA presentations. In particular, our classifications reconstruct and reaggregate the NIPA categories and data in ways that allow the largest and most dynamic components of total public expenditures to emerge. We use the four classifications as complementary perspectives on how public expenditures have behaved over time.

We briefly describe the four classifications below.

### The Functions of Public Expenditures

*Perspective 1: The function of the expenditure.*

The first perspective from which we view public expenditures is their function. This classification scheme categorizes expenditures in the way that usually draws the most attention and public policy analysis—defense, education, health, transportation, and so forth.

Although NIPA provides relatively detailed displays of expenditures by function for federal and state and local expenditures separately, its scheme of national aggregation suffers from two defects. First, its construction mainly reflects a federal perspective, rather than a perspective that combines expenditures by all government jurisdictions. Second, the

---

[4]Kotlikoff (1992) and Auerbach et al. (1994) are authoritative sources on generational accounting. OMB (1993, 1994:9–31) describes the relevance of generational accounting and capital budgeting, as well as the other types of accounting, for the federal budget.

NIPA functional classification is based on public expenditure categories that were relevant during the early years our analysis covers but whose relevance had eroded to some extent by the later years.[5]

Our new classification reaggregates and reconstructs elements of the NIPA functional classification to provide a current national perspective on public expenditures. In keeping with our overall goals, this classification also casts in sharp relief those functions that have shown the most movement or that have been quantitatively most important relative to the whole. At the same time, it allows many smaller, more stable functions with similar purposes to be consolidated, and thus to recede into the background.[6]

## The Jurisdiction That Undertakes the Expenditure

The functional classification of public expenditures is silent on whether an expenditure occurs at the federal or state and local level of government. Hence, an immediate question is, How have these jurisdictions participated in the changes in expenditures that have occurred over time?[7]

*Perspective 2: The jurisdiction that undertakes the expenditure.*

The importance of this politically standard breakdown cannot be overemphasized, since state and local expenditures make up roughly one-third of total public expenditures and a much larger share of domestic expenditures. In addition, state and local expenditures tend to dominate a number of functional categories, such as education, that are the focus of substantial ongoing policy debate.

An important factor in this classification is that jurisdictions are not financially independent in the United States. In particular, the institution of federal grants-in-aid to states and localities is well-entrenched, even though the magnitude of these grants has waxed and waned with political changes in Washington. We shall treat federal grants as an important type of *intergovernmental transfer* in Chapter 3 even though they are not properly regarded as public expenditures per se.

---

[5]See the discussion in Appendix B.

[6]We should note in passing that our analysis, like the NIPA data themselves, only takes account of "first-round" effects of government expenditures—that is, the magnitude of the expenditures themselves—rather than the subsequent effects of the expenditures. These subsequent effects may be more important for the economy than the expenditures, the standard example being effects of federal price supports on farmer incentives.

[7]NIPA treats the state and local sector as a whole. Hence, on the basis of these data, it is not possible to determine whether specific expenditures are undertaken at the state, local, or special-district level. Additional distinctions would not necessarily be useful for our purposes of mapping broad trends in large expenditure categories, however.

## The Economic Type of an Expenditure

Distinctions among economic types of expenditures are founded on their different economic effects and have long been standard in the public-finance literature.

In addition, a major purpose of this report is to view public expenditures in relation to the economy, and the various economic types of expenditure indicate in general terms the private recipients of income from the public expenditure. Thus, this classification scheme connects public expenditures with the economy as a whole.

We now briefly describe each type of expenditure.[8]

*Purchases of goods and services* consist of two components: government-employee compensation for current services, and government purchases of goods and services from businesses and from abroad that are used to produce public goods and services. These expenditures become personal income of government employees' households and sales income of businesses here and abroad. As such, they are a key measure of government's size in the economy.

*Transfer payments* are payments to individuals that augment their households' income or purchasing power and for which the individuals do not render current services. Examples include Social Security, Unemployment Insurance, and Aid to Families with Dependent Children (AFDC). Excluding compensation of government employees, which is included in purchases, transfers are the major type of public expenditure that becomes household income.

*Net interest paid* is the difference between gross interest paid by government and gross interest and dividends it receives. Gross interest payments include expenditures to service outstanding government debt, the result of past borrowing. Gross interest and dividends received includes earnings on government assets in various forms, ranging from balances in social insurance and other trust funds to direct government loans to other sectors and bank balances held by local government entities. These activities lead to income for government creditors and payments from government debtors, in other sectors of the economy.

Finally, *subsidies less current surpluses of government enterprises* is the difference between two types of expenditures that relate to the business sector of the economy. "Subsidies" are monetary grants that government pays to public and private business to modify the supply or price of goods or services. (Major examples are farm and housing subsidies.) Government enterprises function like private businesses and produce goods and services for sale. (Major examples are the U.S. Postal Service, municipal gas and electric companies, and state liquor stores.)

---

[8]For formal definitions of the terms, as used in NIPA, see BEA (1992–1993:M-5–M-13).

The current expenses of these enterprises are subtracted from sales income, and only the "current surplus" of the enterprise is considered part of public expenditures.[9]  Surpluses are netted against subsidies because subsidies augment business income, while surpluses represent the results of substituting public for private supply of goods and services and hence diminish potential business income.  Because any surplus represents a net fee for a government good or service, it is not a withdrawal from the private economy in the same sense as a government receipt with which no good or service is directly associated.  Hence, NIPA classifies these surpluses as "negative expenditures" (BEA, 1988: 6–8).

### The Fund That Pays for the Expenditure

This perspective draws a distinction between social insurance expenditures and regular budget (i.e., non–social insurance) expenditures.  It is the least familiar of our four perspectives, but valuable nonetheless.  Our analysis shows that separating public expenditures by fund is important for understanding how the federal component of public expenditures has behaved over the past 41 years.  Moreover, for the individual citizen, the distinction between funds is highly relevant, since these two budgets represent two social contracts in contemporary American society.  The citizens' view of governments' responsibilities and roles is quite different for the two kinds of funds.

*Perspective 4: The fund that pays for the expenditure.*

**The social insurance budget.**  This budget involves compulsory contributions by private and public employers and employees—for example, the Social Security payroll tax.  Contributions for social insurance programs are part of employers' labor costs and they are deducted from employees' gross earnings.[10]

In return for reduced immediate compensation for their work, employees become eligible for benefits from various social insurance funds at a later time.  Benefits paid from these funds are generally related to the income of individuals from employment or to payments made on their account, whether by themselves or by their employers.[11]  Social insurance disbursements have frequently become a significant component of lifetime financial planning, despite their potential for change by legislation.

**The regular budget.**  The regular budget embodies a complex but loose social contract in which the individual citizen pays and benefits in a vari-

---

[9]Gross receipts of these enterprises are provided in Table 3.9 of BEA (1992–1993).

[10]See the definition of a trust fund in BEA (1988:5).  This definition is also quoted in a somewhat different context in Appendix A.

[11]See BEA (1988:5).  The reason that these payments are only "generally related to . . . the contributions" has to do with the Hospital Insurance component of Medicare.  In this case, the level of benefits paid also depends on whether illness occurs and on its severity.

ety of ways, but without an individually based contract. Compulsory tax payments are made and subsequently allocated by elected officials to a vast array of public expenditures. The taxpayer may or may not approve of these expenditures but, in any case, has no expectation of getting the money back from the government in the future. Whatever current or future benefits the individual receives are mainly unpriced—defense, education, police protection, and so forth. Indeed such benefits cannot, in many instances, be priced, since they accrue from public goods. In these cases, market allocation fails and a prime case for government provision of the good exists.[12]

## SCOPE, DATA, AND METHODS

*The analysis examines total public expenditures between 1952 and 1993.*

In our analysis, we seek to capture behavior of total public expenditures over the period 1952 to 1993. We begin in 1952 for two reasons: First, the data in NIPA for our four major classifications begin in 1952. Second, a series of events occurred in or near 1952 that have affected the subsequent character and trends of public expenditures in profound ways, thus making the year an excellent point of departure for analysis. Specifically,

- Social Security benefits were increased in 1950 for the first time since benefit payments began ten years earlier; 1952 saw the second increase in what was to become a long series of increases that would, in part, drive Social Security expenditures to their current levels.

- In 1953, President Eisenhower announced the "floating D-Day" national defense policy. In practice, this meant that defense expenditures were to fluctuate far less than they had historically and were to remain high in peacetime to support a force that was large, constantly ready, and steadily modernizing.

- By 1952, the first cohorts of the post–World War II baby boom had entered the first grade of the public education system. They and the cohorts that followed were to drive upward many categories of public expenditures, especially those connected with primary and secondary education—the largest single category of state and local expenditures.

- In 1951, the Federal Reserve won full independence from the Treasury Department in setting monetary policy, and the emphasis on low short-term interest rates to facilitate financing the federal debt abated. Eventually, monetary policy would play a significant role in shaping expenditure trends, especially during the later years considered in this analysis.

---

[12]See, for example, Arrow (1969/1983:145–148) and Wolf (1988:20–23) for detailed treatments.

## Data

Each of the expenditure classifications constructed for this report is based on data from NIPA. This choice has shaped our analysis in several ways.

**Advantages of the NIPA data.** The NIPA data have two important advantages for this analysis: First, they are the only statistics that are consistent across our four classification schemes. Second, unlike many other official and semiofficial data sources, the accounts represent the flow of both economic product and income and, as such, are the best representation of the public sector's role in the U.S. economy.[13]

**Limitations of the data.** At the same time, however, using NIPA as our primary data source limits the types of questions we can address fully. Perhaps most important, NIPA's exclusive emphasis is on quarterly or yearly flows in economic quantities, rather than on the quantities' stocks. To take a simple example, annual household *income*, a flow, is reported in NIPA, but annual household *wealth*, a stock, is not. As a result, we cannot fully explain trends in categories of public expenditure where the role of accumulated stocks is important.[14]

In addition, since NIPA is an accounting framework designed to record fully economic activity in terms of public and private flows of product and income, it handles certain aspects of government expenditure in a manner different from frameworks used in budgetary presentations. Hence, our analysis has involved a minimal amount of data reconstruction to bring the NIPA data into line with treatments we consider more useful for our purposes.[15]

*Using data from NIPA has shaped the analysis in several ways.*

---

[13]NIPA uses the term "government expenditures" for transactions between governments and other sectors of the economy—businesses, households, nonprofit institutions, and the rest of the world. In this report, we substitute "public expenditures" to clarify our exclusion of interfund transactions that are included in NIPA's term. In addition, and of equal importance, the alternative term allows us to distinguish between federal "public" expenditures (i.e., transactions between the federal government and other economic sectors, which exclude grants, or "intragovernmental expenditures") and federal "total" expenditures (i.e., federal totals that include grants). Further explanation of these definitions is contained in the appendices.

[14]For instance, explaining in detail how public interest earnings and payments (each a financial flow) have behaved over the past 41 years requires detailed knowledge of how the composition of federal and state and local portfolios (each a stock variable) has changed over the period. Although this information is available in the Federal Reserve's flow-of-funds data, its analysis at a level of detail commensurate with the remainder of the report would take us far afield. Likewise, discussion of the Resolution Trust Corporation's expenditures for deposit insurance on failed thrift institutions is not treated in what follows, since these expenditures recognize and dispose of assets and liabilities rather than reflect flows of economic activity.

[15]These changes are described and explained in the various appendices to this report, particularly Appendix A. The descriptions contain sufficient detail that our calculations can be reproduced from the primary NIPA data, whose integrity has hence been maintained.

## Basic Methods

There are several options for explicating the behavior of long time series of economic variables. The most common methods are to express the series in terms of constant-dollar quantities by using one or another of the deflators constructed by the BEA or the Bureau of Labor Statistics, or in terms of a fraction of another economic aggregate, such as GDP.

**Drawbacks of deflating long time series of public expenditures.** There are technical difficulties in constructing constant-dollar estimates of expenditures over a 40-year period that have to do with changes in taste and quality, coverage of published deflated time series, the significance of price changes, and requirements for viewing public expenditures as part of the larger economy. We treat each of these difficulties in turn.

First, taking account of taste and quality changes when deflating long time series of nominal values is a well-known problem in the economics literature. Since 1952, there have been six revisions of the benchmark year used to calculate implicit price deflators, and, in general, economic magnitudes are roughly comparable only in years near the base year. As the base year is updated, a constant-dollar expenditure series will become progressively more inaccurate for years farthest in the past, as the effects of quality and taste change make themselves increasingly felt.[16] The potential for inaccuracy becomes substantial for a 40-year series.

Second, deflated series are published in NIPA for only two of the four basic types of public expenditures—purchases and subsidies less surpluses of government enterprises. Even for these expenditure types, however, the level of detail in the deflated series is insufficient for presentation of an adequate functional classification. Moreover, the BEA does not provide deflated series for transfer or net interest payments (BEA, 1986:xiii).[17] Hence, the available coverage in constant dollars is not consistent with the scope of our analysis.

---

[16]In particular, unless one is willing to move to a full "hedonic" procedure of index construction, which is not current practice in the government statistics, constant-dollar estimates of expenditures will be biased. For further discussion, see Fisher and Shell (1972) and the essays in Griliches (1971).

[17]It is useful to note that NIPA provides deflated series for product-side components of GDP but fails to do so for income-side components, since deflators cannot be constructed for these components of national income. A simple dimensional argument suggests why this is so: If we deflate aggregate interest or transfer payments, for example, by an index of interest or transfer rates, we arrive at a measure of the time taken to accrue the interest or payments, respectively. In effect, then, we measure *inputs* in these cases, as we would on the product side of GDP, rather than *incomes*, as we wish to do on the income side. Despite its age, Ackley (1961:89–90) seems to present the only complete discussion of this point.

It could be argued that part of an interest-rate change, for example, reflects willingness of bond holders to defer consumption (in effect, an augmentation to a factor of production), while the remainder is an inflation premium (a pure price change). To deflate aggregate interest payments, we would need a procedure to isolate the first of these effects. This procedure would, in effect, deflate goods prices, and we would thus return to a concept that measures output rather than income. Procedures of this sort are conceptually

Third, as we will discuss in Chapter 2, price increases in certain specific functional categories, such as health expenditures, are significant contributors to their trends relative to the economy. Hence, deflating these expenditures, thereby emphasizing their quantity changes, runs the risk of missing a substantial part of the reason for their relative increase.

Finally, deflating expenditures would disrupt the double-entry nominal basis of NIPA, since coverage of both the product and income sides of the economy is available only in nominal terms. Thus, using deflated expenditures would preclude direct examination of the role played by public expenditures and receipts within the private sector and the role of deficits in national saving—major concerns of the analysis in the third report in this series on the U.S. public budget.

**Expressing expenditures as a fraction of GDP.** We have instead chosen to express expenditures as a fraction of GDP, since at the most basic level, our analysis asks how various categories of public expenditure have behaved relative to the economy as a whole. Hence, expressing these categories as a fraction of GDP is one simple means of addressing this basic aim. This procedure is not without its drawbacks, however. In particular, a time series constructed as the ratio of two others will display overall fluctuations brought on by fluctuations in both the numerator and the denominator.[18] Thus, a certain amount of cyclical noise in the economy must be discounted in the trends. We point out these instances in the course of our discussion.

*Expenditures are expressed as a fraction of GDP.*

Likewise, it is important to note that if expenditures are expressed as a fraction of GDP, an expenditure category that increases is, in fact, increasing more rapidly than GDP, with analogous conclusions for categories that are trendless or falling over time. Hence, expenditure categories with trends rising relative to GDP are the main contributors to growth of the public sector.

Finally, expressing expenditures as a fraction of GDP can lead one to think that small changes are not significant. It is useful to remember that in 1993, 1 percent of GDP was equal to $63 billion, and seemingly small relative percentage changes can represent important developments for American society.

---

feasible but are unimplemented thus far. (Indexation of principal and interest payments of Treasury obligations for consumer inflation provides a frequently cited example. See, for example, Federal Reserve Chairman Alan Greenspan's recent remarks on improving the quality of economic measurements (Greenspan, 1994:912).)

[18]For example, when government unemployment benefits increase as a fraction of GDP during a recession, the increase results both because transfers to individuals rise and because GDP falls. Hence, the ratio of transfers to GDP is likely to overstate the magnitude of the fluctuation. Note, too, that in this example movements in the functional category and in GDP reinforce each other to produce the overall trend in the ratio. In general, however, such reinforcement need not occur, and offsetting movements can also be observed.

## A ROAD MAP

The remainder of this report consists of three chapters. In Chapter 2 we present our functional classification of national public expenditures. Chapter 3 exploits classifications by jurisdiction, expenditure type, and type of fund to disaggregate and analyze total public expenditures according to these perspectives. Finally, Chapter 4 summarizes our analysis and contains policy conclusions that emerge from synthesis across the perspectives.

## 2. TRENDS IN U.S. PUBLIC EXPENDITURES: 1952–1993—A FUNCTIONAL PERSPECTIVE

In this chapter we describe trends in total public expenditures in the United States during the past 41 years from the perspective of the function of those expenditures. Adopting this perspective in effect requires that we proceed as if the United States had a single central fisc and general fund.

A functional classification of public expenditures is fraught with legitimate differences in viewpoint about how best to describe what government does. In addition, such a classification must attempt to capture a daunting array of expenditures.[1] Fortunately, NIPA contains a generally acceptable functional classification of expenditures, and we have used this as the basis for our expenditure classification. However, we have reaggregated the elements in a way that highlights large and dynamic expenditure categories while allowing small and more static categories to recede into the background.[2]

Our functional categories and their definitions are:

*Definition of our functional categories*

- *International expenditures:* Primarily defense, but also the conduct of foreign affairs and economic assistance to other nations;

- *Financial expenditures:* Interest paid minus interest earned;

- *Expenditures on general government functions:* Legislative, judicial, and central executive activities, plus financial management expenses for all units of government; retirement expenditures for government employees, net of their public employer contributions; and

- *Domestic expenditures:* The broad category of remaining expenditures that provide for the well-being of the U.S. population.

We begin our discussion with an overview of how these four functional categories have behaved relative to the economy. In the succeeding four subsections, we explore the behavior of each category in greater detail.

---

[1]The budget of the federal government alone has nearly 200,000 accounts, most of which are devoted to several activities. In addition, each of the more than 80,000 other governmental units in the United States maintains its own detailed accounts.

[2]The NIPA functional classification is contained in Tables 315, 316, and 317 of BEA (1992–1993). For greater detail on how we arrived at our classification, as well as its uses, see Appendix B.

## OVERVIEW

*Total public expenditures have grown relative to the economy.*

Figure 2.1 shows total public expenditures by major function as percentages of GDP over the past 41 years. Between 1952 and 1993, combined functional expenditures rose from 26.3 to 33.1 percent of U.S. GDP.

Underlying this increase of 6.8 percentage points are large changes in two major functions: First, the commitment of resources to international purposes—primarily national defense—has been large in constant-dollar terms but has been reasonably steady, in contrast to continuous growth in the economy. Hence, as the economy has grown, this expenditure category has declined over time in relative terms, falling from almost 14 percent of GDP to about 5 percent. During the Korean War, in 1952, international expenditures were more than half of all public expenditures of the United States. Today, they are less than 20 percent.

*International expenditures —primarily national defense— have fallen by more than half.*

Second, domestic expenditures have consistently equaled or outpaced the underlying growth rate of the economy during the past 41 years, thereby increasing their presence in the economy. Domestic expenditures have expanded from 10.4 percent of GDP in 1952 to 24.3 percent in 1993. Most of this increase took place between 1952 and 1975, when defense burdens eased in relative terms. A period of rough stability followed through 1988, after which a fresh surge in domestic expenditures lifted total expenditures to a new high by 1993.

*Domestic expenditures have more than doubled.*

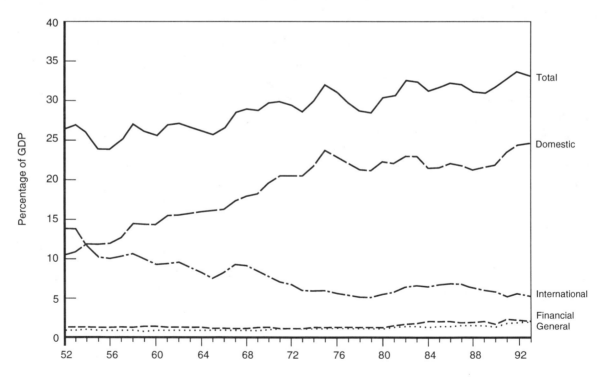

**Figure 2.1—Behavior of Major Functional Categories Relative to GDP**

Financial expenditures were generally steady at about 1 percent of GDP through 1979; between 1979 and 1984, these expenditures rapidly doubled. Financial expenditures are nonprogrammatic. That is, public interest earnings and payments result mainly from the cumulative level of outstanding government debt and its change over time, combined with prevailing interest rates and their movement over time. Although *net* interest payments have been small relative to the economy as a whole, their doubling relative to GDP has contributed to the higher level of total public expenditures since 1979.

*Financial expenditures are small relative to the economy but have doubled relative to GDP.*

Finally, the "General government" category captures the overhead of the government sector. In relative terms it is the smallest of the four aggregate categories. Expenditures for legislative, judicial, and central executive activities and net expenditures for public-employee retirement have grown from 0.8 percent of GDP in 1952 to 1.8 percent in 1993.

We now discuss the components of the "International," "Financial," and "General government" functional categories, before turning to domestic expenditures.

## INTERNATIONAL EXPENDITURES

Figure 2.2 shows the two major subcomponents of international expenditures. Defense expenditures dominate strongly, with peaks during the Korean War, the Vietnam War, and the recent defense buildup.[3]

*Defense expenditures dominate international expenditures.*

### Trends and Cycles in Defense Expenditures

The key to understanding the relative decline in defense expenditures is that growth in the economy has dominated fluctuations in defense expenditures over time; hence, these expenditures have declined as a percentage of GDP. Measured in 1987 dollars, defense purchases have ranged between $180 billion and $300 billion over the past 41 years, as shown in Figure 2.3.[4] They briefly peaked at or near the top of this range during the Korean War (1953) and the Vietnam War (1967), while sustaining the maximum for several years during the crest of the Carter-Reagan defense buildup (1987). However, in those years they amounted to declining shares of GDP: 13.2, 9.0, and 6.4 percent, respectively. The lower bound in constant dollars was reached in the mid-1970s.

*Defense expenditures have declined relative to the economy.*

---

[3]The sharp dip in 1991 in the category of "Other international" expenditures is, in fact, defense-related as well. This category includes both the conduct of foreign affairs and economic assistance to other nations. Financial contributions to the United States from other nations during Operations Desert Shield and Desert Storm were recorded, in effect, as reverse assistance.

[4]Figure 2.3 shows defense purchases in 1987 dollars beginning in 1972, as they appear in BEA (1992–1993: Table 311). For the years between 1952 and 1971, when there was no separate defense-purchases deflator, we used the federal-purchases implicit price deflator.

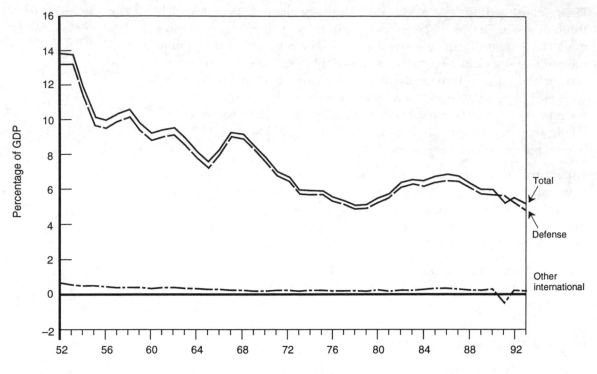

**Figure 2.2—International Expenditures**

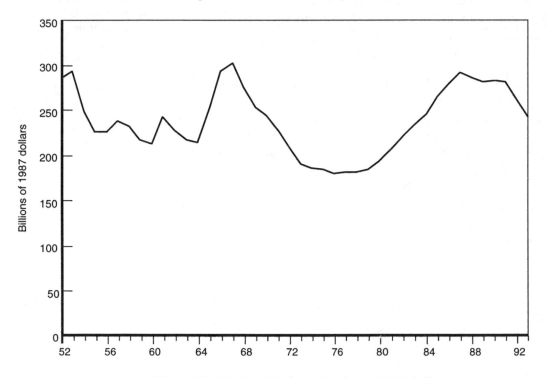

**Figure 2.3—National Defense Purchases (1987 dollars)**

## The Volatility of Defense Expenditures

In addition to their long-term decline relative to the economy, defense expenditures display an interesting secondary trend: substantial volatility relative to GDP. For example, as shown in Figure 2.3, during the 10 years between 1955 and 1965, these expenditures fell by 2.3 percentage points of GDP. As a result of the Vietnam mobilization in 1965, however, the expenditures grew by 1.8 percentage points through 1967, making up 75 percent of the ground lost over 10 years in only 2. Similarly, in the 12 years between 1967 and 1979, defense expenditures fell by 4.1 percentage points of GDP. When the first Reagan administration sustained and ultimately enhanced the military buildup begun in the last year of the Carter administration, however, these expenditures rose by 1.6 percentage points through 1986. Hence, although its effects were more modest than those of the Vietnam mobilization, the Carter-Reagan buildup nonetheless reversed in 7 years nearly 40 percent of the preceding 12-year decline.

**Reasons underlying the volatility.** The reasons behind this volatility are numerous and subject to a variety of interpretations, but at least one stands out: Over much of the time period shown in Figure 2.3, the United States had an acute problem in interpreting Soviet capabilities and intentions. The result was a decades-long cycle in interpretations of the Soviet threat that was conditioned by contemporary Soviet behavior, colored by perceptual and ideological proclivities of U.S. decisionmakers, and influenced by the exigencies of U.S. domestic politics.

*The volatility of defense expenditures reflects cycles in U.S. interpretation of the threat.*

A brief review of the period's rhetoric illustrates this point. For example, the North Vietnamese were viewed as "Soviet proxies," and the "domino theory" of Soviet expansion thus justified escalation of the Vietnam War to serve the broader purposes of containment, as it had justified U.S. actions in Korea earlier, with a rapid increase in defense expenditures the result. Likewise, the Soviet invasion of Afghanistan in 1979 under the rubric of the Brezhnev Doctrine, combined with a perceived "window of [strategic-force] vulnerability" following a "decade of neglect" in U.S. defense preparedness during the 1970s, led to a subsequent expansion in expenditures. Hence, in many ways the volatility of U.S. defense expenditures is the fiscal reification of underlying volatility in Soviet behavior and U.S. interpretations of that behavior.[5]

**Implications of the volatility.** The volatility of defense expenditures has a number of important implications for understanding their role in the public sector. These expenditures are virtually unique in the degree to which they have a substantial—and arguably unknowable—perceptual

---

[5]Perceptual influences on the assessment of military threats have been historically pervasive. For an excellent survey of how participants in the two world wars perceived threats prior to hostilities, see May (1984). Wark (1985) analyzes how British intelligence perceived the German threat before World War II.

component ("the threat") at their base.[6] As the remainder of this section will illustrate, other categories of expenditures are driven by variables such as the demographics of the U.S. population and interest rates, which may swing broadly and decisively but which provide much less leeway for interpretation. Hence, when world events cause a broad reappraisal of the external threat, as is now occurring, defense expenditures come to the fore as an obvious candidate for budgetary cuts. Moreover, calls for such cuts may precede events, rather than coinciding with them, since at least some decisionmakers are likely to hold a minimalist interpretation of the threat.

### The Mix of Defense Expenditures

Like the overall trend in defense expenditures, the mix of these expenditures has changed in interesting ways over the period under review. The three main subcategories of defense expenditures are "Procurement," "Research, development, test, and evaluation (RDT&E)," and "Operations." Expenditures on the first two subcategories contribute to determining the size, structure, modernity, and technological characteristics of U.S. forces, while expenditures on operations affect the forces' readiness and sustainability.

*Historically, procurement and research accounted for 40 percent of defense outlays; operations has accounted for the rest.*

Time trends for procurement, RDT&E, and other defense expenditures are shown in Figures 2.4a and 2.4b. Figure 2.4a shows each subcategory of expenditure as a percentage of GDP, while Figure 2.4b shows each as a percentage of total DoD expenditures.[7] Trends across the subcategories of expenditure have been similar since the Korean War, with roughly 40 percent of total defense expenditures going to procurement and research and 60 percent to all other accounts. Although all subcategories of defense expenditures increased during the Vietnam War, their rough shares remained the same.

Following this peak, reductions in total expenditures relative to GDP were concentrated in procurement through the late 1970s, when the shares shifted dramatically to 30 percent for procurement and RDT&E versus 70 percent for current operations and pay accounts. The buildup in defense expenditures that then followed through the late 1980s was concentrated in procurement and RDT&E until the historical 40–60 split

---

[6]This statement is agnostic as to the reality of that threat. It merely notes that regardless of what Soviet intentions and capabilities, for example, actually were, there was ample opportunity for them to be interpreted and filtered by U.S. decisionmakers.

[7]The panels of Figure 2.4 are based on Table 6.11 in Comptroller, OSD (1987) and OMB (1994b). The total in Figure 2.4a is less than that shown in Figure 2.2 because Figure 2.4a excludes expenditures of federal agencies that are included in NIPA's National Defense category.

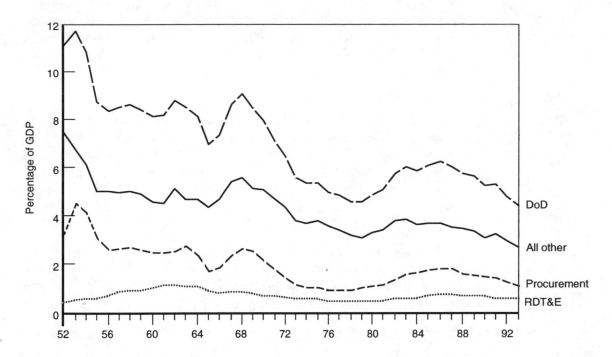

**Figure 2.4a—Department of Defense Outlays Relative to GDP**

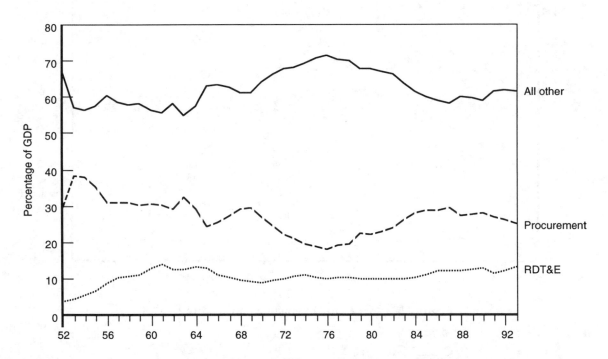

**Figure 2.4b—Department of Defense Outlays by Type as a Percentage of Total Outlays**

was reattained. Finally, the post–Cold-War decline in defense expenditures held procurement and RDT&E roughly constant, at least through 1993.[8]

### Other International Expenditures

The remainder of U.S. international expenditures consists of two functions—"Foreign affairs and international activities" and "Foreign economic assistance," as shown in Figure 2.5.[9] The aggregate magnitude of these expenditures has been small. Indeed, taken together, international nondefense expenditures have amounted to only a little over 0.3 percentage point of GDP, or about one cent on every dollar of U.S. total public expenditures in 1992.

Following the conclusion of the Marshall Plan in the late 1940s, foreign economic assistance declined steadily relative to GDP through the late 1960s, remained low in relative terms throughout the 1970s, and has risen only slightly in recent years.

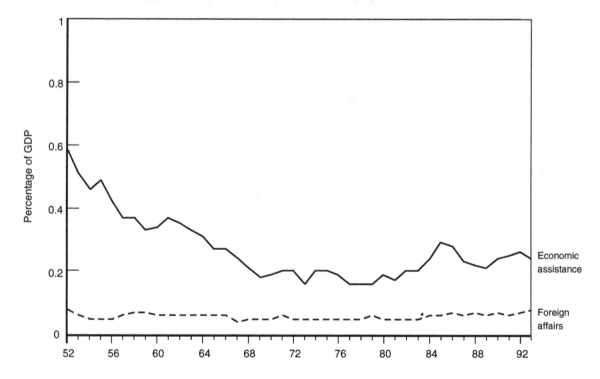

**Figure 2.5—Nondefense International Expenditures**

_____

[8]For an extended discussion of the cyclical defense investment record in this century, including advocacy of a future share for procurement closer to 50 percent of the total, see Korb (1993).

[9]Note that the "reverse assistance" to the United States that was noted above has been excluded in this figure to bring out the long-run trends in these functions.

Expenditures on foreign affairs and international activities have been small and steady over the period.

## FINANCIAL EXPENDITURES

Figure 2.6 shows gross interest payments and earnings at all levels of government, together with their difference—net interest payments.[10]

Two major events drove the trends shown on this figure: The first was the Federal Reserve's announcement on October 6, 1979, that it would no longer seek to regulate interest rates directly, but would instead concentrate on controlling the money supply.[11] A rapid escalation of real interest rates quickly followed. The increase in net interest payments through about 1984 mainly reflects effects of these higher real interest rates on refinancing existing federal debt.

*Net interest payments were a steady 1 percent of GDP until high interest rates after 1979 quickly doubled them.*

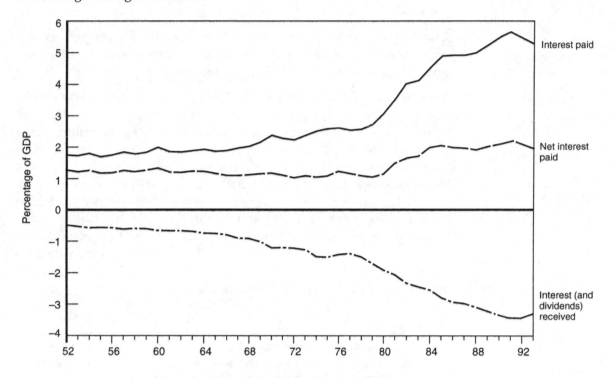

**Figure 2.6—Financial Expenditures**

---

[10]Since the functional perspective of expenditures assumes a unitary public fund, only the net figure is relevant here, strictly speaking. Gross government interest payments and receipts primarily result from principal held in social insurance trust funds—an "interfund" government transaction treated in detail in the next chapter. We show gross totals in Figure 2.6 for reference purposes.

[11]See Mussa (1994:81–144) and Stein (1988:294–306) for discussion of policy changes at the Federal Reserve during the 1980s. Then–Federal Reserve Chairman Paul Volcker has said that the Fed's emphasis on money-supply control began to weaken in the fall of 1982 due to institutional changes that distorted the various definitions of money, particularly M1. (See Volcker, 1994:149; Mussa, 1994:87 gives the then prevailing definition of M1.) It is plausible that the Fed's attention thereafter returned to interest rates.

Second, and in tandem with this policy measure, the large federal deficits in the latter half of the 1980s further increased the stock of liabilities subject to the higher interest rates, causing net interest payments to keep pace with growth in the economy during this period.

## GENERAL GOVERNMENT EXPENDITURES

Figure 2.7a shows total expenditures for "General government" and its two major subcomponents, "Central activities" and "Net retirement."

*Central activities expanded modestly in two stages— from 1968 through 1975 and after 1988.*

The first subcomponent, central activities, denotes expenditures for legislative, judicial, and central executive activities, along with financial management expenses for all units of government.[12] Central activities were 0.9 percent of GDP in 1952 and 1.2 percent in 1993, with their growth occurring over two periods—from 1968 through 1975, and after 1988.

The second subcomponent, retirement expenditures for government employees, is shown net of public employer contributions.[13] This category is small and has grown since the mid-1970s.

For reference purposes, Figure 2.7b shows gross retirement expenditures and government employer retirement contributions, which are deducted from gross retirement expenditures to arrive at net expenditures. We make this deduction because government employer retirement contributions already appear as interfund transactions in the international and domestic categories of expenditures, where they are paid as part of governments' labor expenses to the appropriate social insurance funds. To include these interfund expenditures within these categories and their equivalent again in the government category, where the payout to immediate beneficiaries occurs, would result in double counting within total public expenditures. To avoid this double counting, we count retirement expenditures net of interfund transactions.[14]

---

[12]Ideally, judicial expenditures would be included among domestic expenditures, but they are not separately identified within NIPA.

[13]As with net interest payments, this chapter's assumption of a single central fund eliminates the gross interfund transactions as separate categories.

[14]Deducting government employer contributions from each of the detailed international and domestic functional categories, although technically appropriate, would revise a large amount of data to eliminate the interfund expenditures. Therefore, we adopt the convention of adjusting in one place and use "net" retirement. For further details, see Appendix A.

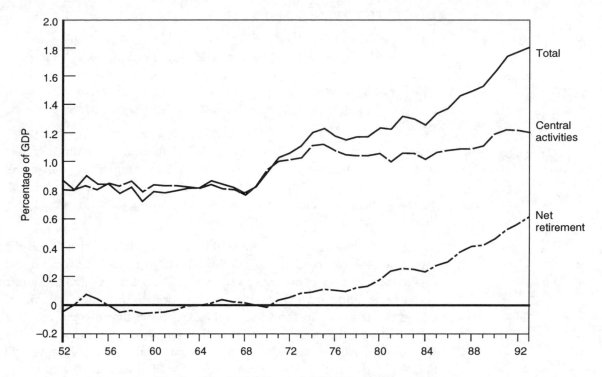

**Figure 2.7a—Total General Government Expenditures**

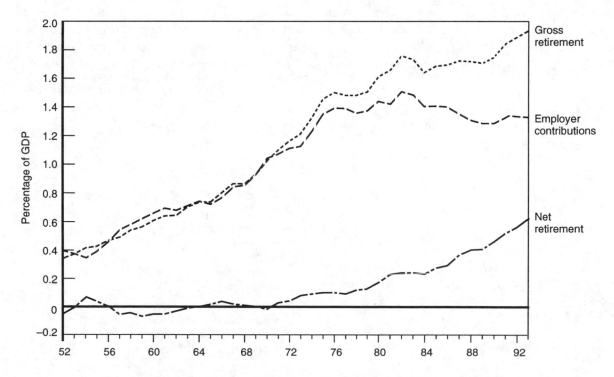

**Figure 2.7b—Components of Net Government Retirement Expenditures**

## DOMESTIC EXPENDITURES

The fourth functional category of expenditures is "Domestic expenditures." Public expenditures for domestic programs have expanded much more rapidly than the economy as a whole—from 10.4 percent of GDP in 1952 to 24.3 percent in 1993. We have defined a comprehensive set of functional categories, shown in Table 2.1, to display trends in these expenditures.

*Definitions of domestic expenditure categories.*

"Basic programs" are those that have traditionally involved direct delivery of public services, mainly through local and state government. For example, basic programs typically fund the local public school, police station, jail, and firehouse, as well as the public hospital and health department, streets, and highways.

The next three categories—support of individuals, the economy, and the labor force—have traditionally been oriented more toward financial and service-based support of targeted individuals, businesses, and economic activities than toward actual delivery of services to the public. "Support of individuals" has historically emphasized providing income or other supporting services for veterans, the blind and deaf, and the poor. Over the period considered in this report, programs for the elderly, especially Social Security, and for the poor have come to dominate the subcategory.

"Support of the economy" includes a collection of functions that are usually addressed separately—agriculture, natural resources, economic regulation and information services, urban renewal, cultural and recreational services, and so forth. These expenditures are combined here because they relate, for the most part, to performance of the economy and because they are relatively small.

"Support of the labor force" is a collection of functions closely related to employment and employability and has come to be dominated in large measure by unemployment insurance.

Table 2.1

FUNCTIONAL CATEGORIES OF DOMESTIC PUBLIC EXPENDITURES

Basic Programs
  Education
  Health
  Transportation
  Civilian safety

Support Programs
  Support of individuals
  Support of the economy
  Support of the labor force

Other Programs
  Utilities and commercial activities
  Unallocable

Finally, the "Other" category contains commercial activities undertaken by government at all levels, along with unallocable expenditures of state and local governments.[15]

We begin by considering the 41-year trends in our most aggregated categories—"Basic programs," "Support programs," and "Other programs." Then we turn our attention to the behavior of their subcomponents. In the course of the discussion, we suggest factors that seem to have stimulated growth in various functions.

### Domestic Expenditures: An Overview

Figure 2.8 shows the behavior of all U.S. domestic public expenditures relative to GDP since 1952, as well as the behavior of their major functional categories.

Total domestic expenditures increased steadily relative to GDP through 1975, as did all three of the category's subcomponents in varying degrees. The total increased from 10.4 percent to 23.9 percent of GDP between 1952 and 1975, with the increase of 13.5 percentage points divided almost equally between basic programs (up 6.5 percentage points) and support programs (up 6.0 points); the "Other" subcategory increased by just under 1 percentage point.

*Domestic expenditures have grown from 10 percent of GDP to almost 25 percent.*

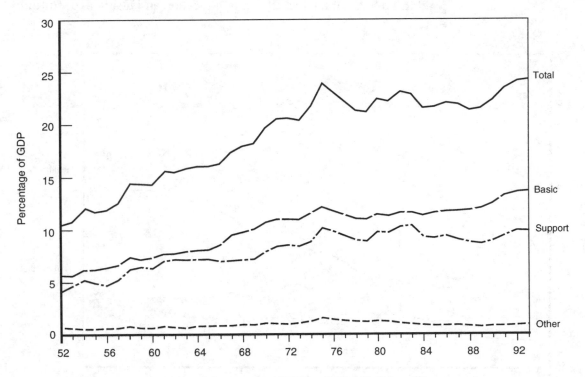

**Figure 2.8—Functional Categories of Domestic Public Expenditures**

---

[15]For further explanation of these domestic expenditure categories, see Appendix B.

After 1975, however, basic programs stabilized at around 11.5 percent of GDP, as did support programs at under 10 percent. Hence, total domestic expenditures also remained nearly constant relative to GDP through 1988.

In 1989, after more than a decade of stability, both basic and support programs again began to expand much more quickly than the economy, pushing domestic expenditures to a new high of 24.3 percent of GDP by 1993.

### Basic Programs

Figure 2.9 shows the four major subcategories of basic domestic expenditures: "Education," "Health," "Transportation," and "Civilian safety."

*The dominant components of basic domestic expenditures have changed over time.*

Figure 2.9 captures the types of shifts that have occurred in domestic spending for basic programs. In particular, the figure draws our attention to four time periods.

The first period extended through 1965. During this time, the drivers of relative growth in basic expenditures were education and, to a far lesser extent, transportation.

The second period opened with the authorization of Medicare and Medicaid in 1965. Over the next 10 years, education and health expenditures

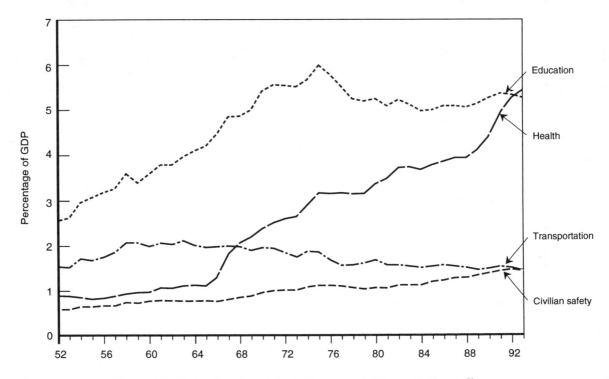

**Figure 2.9—Subcategories of Basic Programs in Domestic Expenditures**

grew rapidly relative to GDP, fueling the overall expansion of basic expenditures. During this period, spending on civilian safety also increased slightly, but transportation expenditures declined.

The third period, 1975–1988, witnessed two major substitutions in basic expenditures. The first, and larger, substitution occurred with the 1-percentage-point drop in education expenditures, following the peak of the post–World War II baby boom, and a similarly sized increase in health expenditures. The second, smaller, substitution involved nearly a 0.5-percentage-point decline in transportation expenditures and an increase in civilian-safety expenditures of the same magnitude. The effect of these substitutions, taken together, was to maintain basic expenditures roughly constant relative to GDP over the period.

Finally, a rapid increase in health expenditures and a slight rise in education expenditures between 1988 and 1993 drove domestic expenditures to a new high by the latter year.

We now consider each of these functional categories in more detail, linking the patterns of their evolution, when appropriate, to basic demographic and economic factors.

**Education.** Historically, public expenditures on education have been the largest component of basic programs. Figure 2.10 shows expenditure trends relative to GDP for various types of education.

The categories shown at the bottom of the chart have played a small role in total education expenditures. Veterans' education peaked in the 1970s, reflecting benefits related to the Vietnam War; the "Other" category, which includes programs ranging from federal research sponsorship to local libraries, has been small and steady.

*Education expenditures rose rapidly until the mid-1970s, dipped, then rose again. Post–World War II birth rates have generally shaped the expenditure trend.*

Higher education rose steadily until the 1970s and has been stable thereafter. Part of this rise is explained by the arrival of successive baby-boom cohorts, as described below. However, in interpreting this trend, it is important to bear in mind that only public expenditures for higher education are shown. In particular, student-paid tuition and related charges appear as personal consumption expenditures in NIPA. Since tuition and charges have grown over time, the flattening of the trend partly reflects an increased shifting of costs toward students.[16]

The bulk of public education expenditures has occurred at the primary and secondary (K–12) levels. Between 1952 and 1990, expenditures per primary and secondary school student in 1987 dollars rose almost linearly from $1,291 to $4,584.

*Primary and secondary education consumed the lion's share of education expenditures.*

---

[16]Between 1960 and 1990, tuition and charges rose from 0.1 percent of GDP to 0.4 percent. (See BEA (1992–1993: Table 309B, Line 39).)

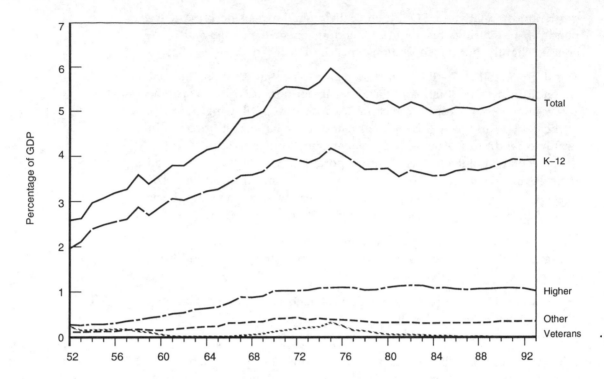

**Figure 2.10—Expenditures for Public Education**

In general, the shape of the expenditure trend reflects the arrival of successive cohorts of children associated with the post–World War II baby boom and its aftermath (Figure 2.11). In 1952, the first of these cohorts was six years of age and entered the first year of primary school. Public school enrollment escalated sharply for nearly the next two decades. Between 1952 and 1971, the year of their peak, K–12 enrollments increased by 3.3 percent annually, and expenditures for elementary and secondary education likewise increased in relative terms. The expenditures continued to expand through 1974 at a slower rate that roughly equaled growth in the economy, despite a slight downturn in enrollments.[17]

Between 1976 and 1981, however, primary and secondary school enrollments declined sharply at an annual rate of 2 percent, and expenditures decreased relative to GDP. Enrollments continued to decline through 1984 but did so at an attenuated rate that roughly equaled the rate of decline between 1971 and 1974. Expenditures during this period kept pace with the growth in GDP. Finally, after 1984, enrollment rose again, as a result of the baby boom's "echo," and expenditures again increased relative to GDP.

---

[17]Note that the sharp rise in education expenditures relative to GDP in 1975 (Figure 2.10) was brought on by the severe recession of that year and the consequent drop in GDP, rather than by an increase in the expenditures themselves.

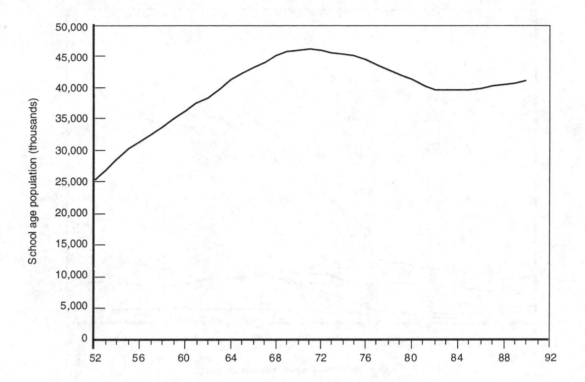

Source: National Center for Education Statistics (various years).

**Figure 2.11—Trends in the School-Age Population**

**Health.** From their modest pre-1965 level, health expenditures have increased rapidly in relative terms; they surpassed the level of education expenditures in 1993. Figure 2.12 shows the components of this category.

The contrast among the four programs shown in Figure 2.12 is almost as dramatic as the rate of growth in total health expenditures. The "Health and hospitals" and "Veterans" categories contain programs in which government itself produces and delivers health services. Hence, the costs of public health departments, as well as those of local and veterans' hospitals, have remained subject to traditional measures of public budgetary control.[18] Put another way, the amount of service supplied has been constrained by the prior authorization of limited resources.

*Since the authorization of Medicare and Medicaid in 1965, health expenditures have risen from about 1 percent of GDP to more than 5 percent in 1993.*

---

[18]The "Health and hospitals" category reflects only public expenditures and, in particular, omits charges paid by beneficiaries or on their behalf. These charges have increased from 0.2 percent of GDP in 1960 to 0.9 percent in 1990 (BEA (1992–1993), Table 309B, Line 39). Thus, the decline shown in Figure 2.12 mainly reflects shifting of costs to beneficiaries—or, more accurately, to third-party payers for health care services.

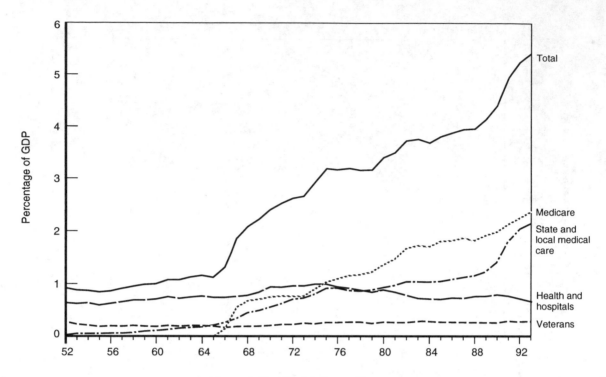

**Figure 2.12—Health Expenditures**

*Medicare and Medicaid made the government responsible for health care costs but provided limited means for controlling type, quantity, and price of service.*

*Increase in the size of the eligible population and rising costs of health care services drive the increases in Medicare and Medicaid.*

The new programs authorized in 1965—Medicare for the elderly and Medicaid for the poor—created eligibility for designated individuals to demand services from the existing public and private health care system while bearing few of the costs themselves.[19] These programs have placed government in much the same position as private businesses and health insurers, as well as public and private providers of health care. That is, the government is liable for health care costs, but it has limited ability to control the type, quantity, and price of services delivered.

In the broadest terms, Medicare and Medicaid expenditures have risen for two reasons: increase in the size of the population eligible for benefits under these government programs, and increase in the costs of purchasing health care services for the eligible population from the private sector. Although eligible populations have risen both absolutely and relatively, the rising cost of health care services has been the dominant factor.

There is no consensus about the causes of these increases. Commonly suggested explanations include the following:[20]

---

[19]In addition to Medicaid after 1965, "State and local medical care" includes traditional, locally provided programs of medical assistance for the poor, blind, deaf, and disabled.

[20]See Newhouse (1992), which discusses each explanation for rising costs in detail. See also Weisbrod (1991).

- Increased health costs associated with an aging U.S. population;

- The spread of medical insurance, leading to a reduced or near-zero price to the consumer of medical services in the face of fairly high elasticity of demand;

- Increased U.S. household income, leading to increased consumption of all normal goods, including medical care;

- Physicians' discretion in treating relatively uninformed consumers ("supplier-induced" demand); and

- Lower productivity in medical services, relative to other sectors of the economy, and sufficiently inelastic consumer demand to lead to increased expenditures.

However, a recent analysis by Newhouse (1992) is pessimistic about the degree to which these commonly adduced factors can explain the full increase in health costs. Indeed, although the estimate is subjective, Newhouse concludes that the five factors, taken together, account for well under half, and perhaps less than a quarter, of the increase in expenditures for medical care since 1940.

Newhouse suggests that the lion's share of the increase in public and private health expenditures can be attributed to technological change in medical services. In this instance, technological change amounts to increased capabilities for treatment, implemented both by new types of physical capital and by new medical procedures. Put another way, advances in medical science and technology have led to an increased number of medical products and services, broadly construed, that are available to consumers through physicians, who act as consumers' agents. Because these commodities are newly available, previously unrealized consumer demand has manifested itself, and the quality of care has presumably improved.

*Growing Medicare and Medicaid costs reflect general increases in health care costs, largely stimulated by technological change in medical services.*

In sum, growth in public expenditures for health since the initiation of Medicare and Medicaid is part of the much broader rise in health care costs throughout American society—a phenomenon of immense importance that has complex and controversial causes.

**Transportation.** Expenditures for transportation infrastructure make up the third major category of basic domestic expenditures and are shown relative to GDP in Figure 2.13. Construction and maintenance of highways and streets dominate public expenditures within this category, despite some increase in rail and mass transit expenditures over the past 20 years. Expenditures on air and water transport have been small but steady.

*Highway construction and maintenance dominate transportation expenditures.*

Highway maintenance and other operational expenditures have made up a nearly steady 0.5 percent of GDP, while investment in new highways and streets constitutes the volatile component of the aggregate trend. Therefore, new investment can be approximated by subtracting

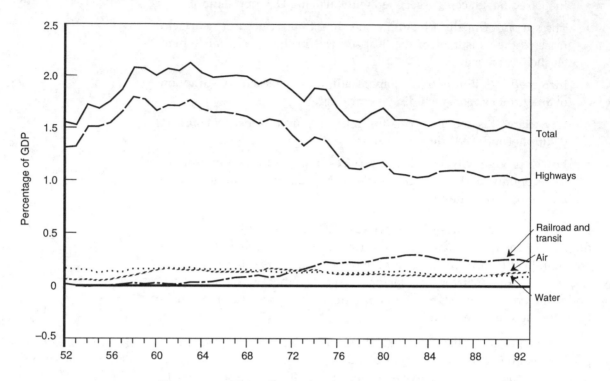

**Figure 2.13—Expenditures for Transportation**

0.5 percentage point from the time series shown in Figure 2.13. Investment in highways and streets made up 0.8 percent of GDP in 1952, rose to a peak of 1.2 percent in 1958, and fell to 0.5 percent in 1982, where it remained through 1993.[21]

Two factors have influenced the behavior of expenditures on highways and streets relative to the economy over the past 40 years. First, receipts from excise taxes on gasoline and other motor fuels are a major source of funds for road construction and maintenance. Second, federal grants are available to match state and local revenues for certain eligible projects.

*Expenditures on highways rose rapidly after authorization of the Interstate Highway System in 1957, then fell sharply after the oil price shocks in the 1970s.*

Within the context of these factors, two events have shaped highway expenditures over the years: First, authorization of the Interstate Highway System in 1957 stimulated a major nationwide construction effort throughout the 1960s. Second, major increases in oil prices occurred in 1973 and 1979. Motor-fuel excise taxes are based on the *volume* of fuel sold rather than on *revenue* deriving from the sale. Hence, if a price increase reduces consumer demand and tax rates are stable, tax revenues will decrease, and conversely. Higher fuel prices also motivated consumers in the 1970s to replace their cars with more fuel-efficient models.

---

[21]See BEA (1992–1993: Table 506, Line 44).

Because of this substitution, the effective tax rate per mile driven fell as the stock of vehicles turned over. Finally, these effects on tax revenues occurred at a time when highway construction costs generally were rising rapidly, due in part to petroleum-based factors of production in highway construction and repair.

The consequence of these developments was a reduction in expenditures on highways from 1972 through 1982. After 1982, tax-rate increases and falling oil prices were sufficient to stabilize highway expenditures relative to GDP. However, the long-term result was reduced infrastructure investment and maintenance in the 1980s, compared with the period before the oil price increases.

**Civilian safety.** Expenditures for civilian safety make up the final category of basic domestic expenditures. As Figure 2.14 shows, these expenditures overall have grown substantially relative to the economy since 1952; however, the growth has not been uniform across subcategories. Fire protection has required a steady 0.2 percent of GDP; police protection rose from 0.4 to 0.6 percent of GDP in a single surge between 1965 and 1975; finally, corrections drifted slowly upward to 0.2 percent of GDP before nearly doubling during the 1980s.

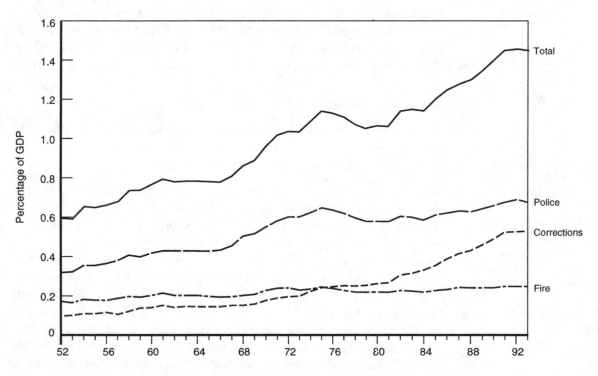

Figure 2.14—Expenditures for Civilian Safety

*Police expenditures increased rapidly between 1965 and 1975. These expenditures are strongly influenced by demographic trends, since arrests are concentrated among the young.*

*Expenditures for corrections rose in the 1980s, mainly reflecting recent changes in sentencing practices.*

***Police expenditures.*** Earlier, we noted effects of the postwar baby boom on expenditures for public primary and secondary education. In general, the baby boom had a parallel, but delayed, effect on police expenditures. The size of the population between 13 and 29 years of age makes a substantial difference in the number of arrests that occur, since all else being equal, individuals are most likely to be arrested between these ages.[22] Thus, until the population between these ages peaked in the 1970s, expenditures on police grew.

***Corrections expenditures.*** On an intuitive level, one might expect these changes in the U.S. age structure to account for the increase in corrections expenditures shown in Figure 2.14, since some fraction of those arrested are eventually incarcerated. Nonetheless, recent research indicates that age-structure changes account for only about 20 percent of the increase in these expenditures. By far the strongest determinant of the increased inmate population is the higher rate of imprisonment for crimes committed in recent years. Tougher practices of judges and prosecutors account for fully 51 percent of the increase in prison admissions after 1973 (Langan, 1991:1572).

In addition, more stringent enforcement of parole and probation provisions has helped to swell the inmate population. For example, courts and parole boards returned 10 percent of the parole population to prison in 1974 for various infractions; by 1986, this figure had increased to 24 percent. Thus, the rise in corrections expenditures mainly reflects changes that have occurred in sentencing practices during recent years.

**Support Programs**

*Expenditures for support of individuals rose sharply between 1952 and 1975, then stabilized. Expenditures for support of the economy and the labor force have been basically static since 1960.*

The second major group of domestic expenditures is "Support programs"—for individuals, for the economy, and for the labor force. Expenditures for these functions are shown in Figure 2.15.

The preceding discussion suggests that each major component of basic domestic expenditures had its own momentum and timing after 1952. The support programs have behaved differently. Only expenditures for programs that support individuals have grown significantly. This growth took place essentially continuously until 1975, and the expenditures have sustained a steady, high level relative to the economy since that time. Although other categories of support programs were somewhat lower in the 1950s than later, their most notable characteristic is that very little change has occurred in each during the past three decades. Finally, it is worth noting a point that we make in detail below, namely, that the great preponderance of these expenditures consists of

---

[22]For example, between 1964 and 1990, 63 percent of all arrests involved suspects in this age range.

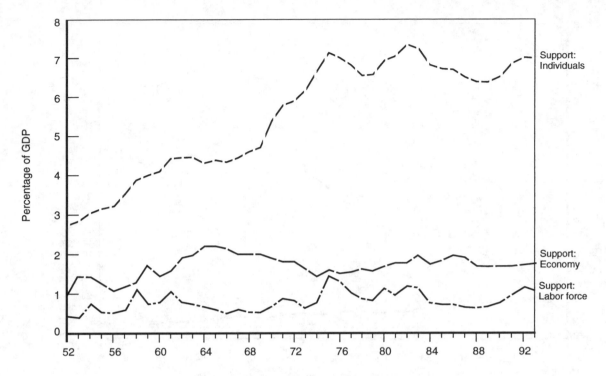

**Figure 2.15—Expenditures for Support Programs**

transfer payments and that only a small portion goes toward purchases of goods and services to administer the transfers.[23]

**Support of individuals.** Historically, public expenditures for support of individuals have been devoted to income support for targeted groups, mainly veterans, the disabled, the elderly, and the poor.[24] The total for this category, along with its five major components, is shown in Figure 2.16.

Two types of support programs have grown over the past 41 years— Social Security for the elderly, and welfare and social services for the poor. In contrast, veterans' disability and survivors' compensation have declined steadily, and Railroad Retirement has been relatively insignificant and static. Supplemental Security Income, the successor to a host of long-standing programs for the blind, deaf, and elderly poor, has also changed little. Thus, the discussion that follows focuses on Social Security and welfare.

*Growth in Social Security for the elderly and in welfare and social services for the poor accounts for a major part of the growth in support programs.*

---

[23]See, for example, Figure 3.9a and its accompanying discussion.

[24]The same targeted groups have also been beneficiaries of other programs. For example, veterans have also received education and health benefits, which were discussed as components of the relevant basic programs. "Support of individuals" contains programs where the form of assistance is general in nature and delivered as social services, transfer payments, or cash-equivalent benefits (e.g., food stamps).

36

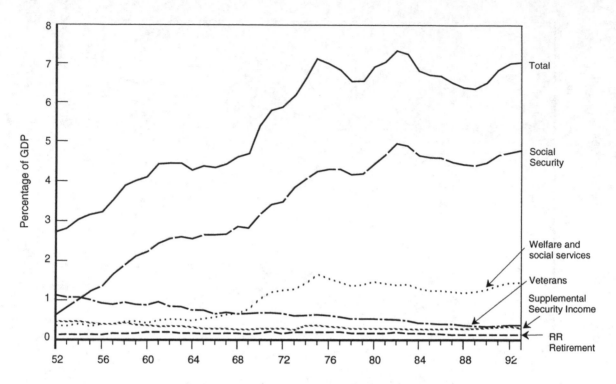

**Figure 2.16—Support of Individuals**

*Social Security*. The "graying of America" has become a fashionable topic in recent years, and the proportion of the population over age 64 has indeed risen—from 8.4 percent in 1952 to 12.7 percent in 1993. As demographers are quick to state, this proportional aging is mainly the result of a long-term downward trend in total fertility that began during the last century and was only temporarily interrupted by the postwar baby boom (Shryock, Siegel, and Associates, 1973:247).

Although the share of the population over 64 has grown during the past 41 years, this increase cannot, in itself, explain the *eightfold* increase in Social Security expenditures relative to GDP during that period. Rather, broadened Social Security coverage and increased benefit payments have been the major drivers of cost growth in the program.

The broadening of Social Security coverage over time is suggested on a qualitative level in Table 2.2, which shows the years in which various occupational groups were brought into the system (Chin, 1983; OMB, 1990:227). The table shows a striking expansion of the program since its inception.

Table 2.2

YEAR OF SOCIAL SECURITY COVERAGE FOR VARIOUS OCCUPATIONAL
GROUPS

| Year | Occupational Group |
|------|--------------------|
| 1935 | • Workers in commerce and industry |
| 1950 | • Employed farm and domestic workers<br>• Nonfarm self-employed, excluding doctors, lawyers, and other professionals |
| 1954 | • Self-employed farmers and other farm workers<br>• Miscellaneous self-employed professionals<br>• Optional for ministers |
| 1956 | • Lawyers and dentists<br>• All professions except doctors and federal employees |
| 1965 | • Doctors |
| 1983 | • Nonprofit organizations<br>• Withdrawal of state and municipal employees prevented |
| 1984 | • Federal civilian employees hired after 1983 |

The table does not quantify the rate at which the number of Social Security beneficiaries has increased. Figure 2.17 shows the number of beneficiaries of the Old-Age and Survivors' Insurance (OASI) Trust Fund between 1940 and 1989. The figure confirms the qualitative conclusion suggested by the table. Between 1950 and 1989, Social Security beneficiaries increased by 6.1 percent per year. The number of Social Security beneficiaries during this period expanded more rapidly than the pool of those aged 62 and over, thus suggesting that the "lateral" expansion in coverage shown in Table 2.2 outstripped the coverage expansion brought on by aging alone.[25]

*Between 1950 and 1989, the number of Social Security beneficiaries grew more rapidly than the pool of those eligible.*

Figure 2.17 also suggests that while the number of beneficiaries was increasing rapidly, the average monthly benefit paid was also increasing rapidly in both nominal and constant-dollar terms. In particular, nominal monthly benefits increased at just short of 7 percent per year, and constant-dollar benefits increased by almost 2 percent per year. The legislated benefit increases came in two stages, the first during the 1950s and the second in the 1970s. Growth in monthly benefit payments during the 1950s resulted from "grandfathering" current benefit recipients when the benefit paid to new recipients increased. In contrast, growth in the 1970s resulted from several large annual increases that well exceeded the rate of inflation, then from the full indexation, and indeed overindexation, of monthly benefits to the inflation rate.[26]

*Since 1940, the average monthly Social Security benefit has grown by almost 2 percent per year in constant dollars.*

---

[25]Eligibility for discounted benefits at age 62 began in 1961.

[26]See Chin (1983) for details.

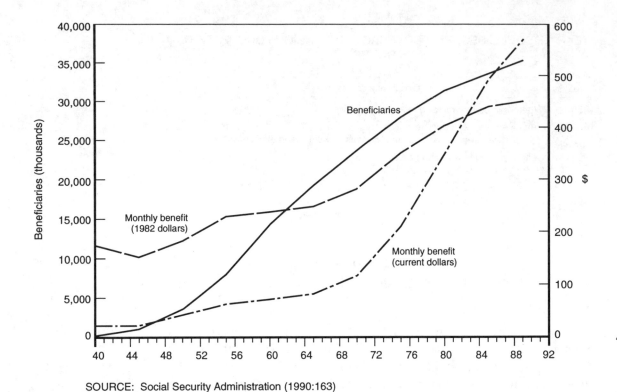

SOURCE: Social Security Administration (1990:163)

**Figure 2.17—Number of Social Security Beneficiaries and Their Average Monthly Benefit**

*Welfare and social services.* The other major component of support for individuals consists of a variety of income-transfer programs and social services. The best known of these programs are Aid to Families with Dependent Children (AFDC) and the Food Stamp program. Figure 2.18 shows expenditures for these programs and for the residual "Other programs" category. (About two-thirds of the expenditures in the latter were to provide services rather than transfer payments.)

*Growth in welfare and social service expenditures occurred mainly between 1965 and 1975. Cyclical expansion has occurred during recent recessions, especially in food-stamp use.*

The major growth in welfare and social services occurred during the decade between the initiation of the Great Society program in 1965 and the recession in 1975. As the trend in AFDC expenditures illustrates, concern for the poor became intense in the mid-1960s but was attenuated substantially in the mid-1970s, at least when measured by expenditure patterns.

Periods of rapid growth in this subcategory have occurred during recent recessions: in 1969–1971, in 1974–1975, selectively in 1980–1983, and finally in 1990–1992. This countercyclical behavior is especially evident in the Food Stamp program. Thus, at least on a qualitative level, food stamps act as an "automatic stabilizer" in the economy, much like Unemployment Insurance.

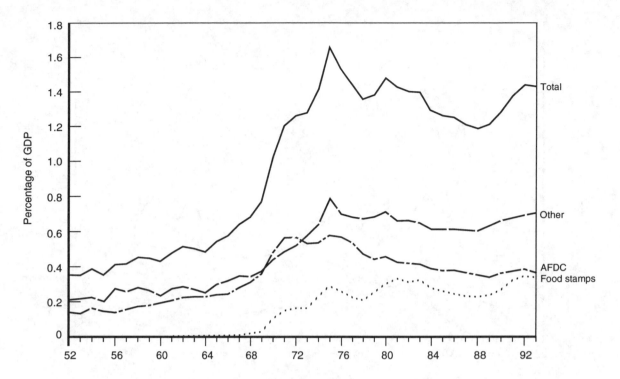

**Figure 2.18—Expenditures for Welfare and Social Services**

**Support of the economy.** This subcategory contains a large number of separate, small functions that relate in some fashion to operations of the economy.[27] The reason for aggregation is demonstrated by Figure 2.19, which shows total expenditures for the subcategory and its three components. The overall total has drifted between 1.5 and 2.2 percent of GDP for the past 30 years.

*Expenditures in support of the economy have fluctuated between 1.5 and 2.2 percent of GDP for the past 30 years.*

The collection of programs in "Agriculture, natural resources, and energy" varies mainly because of fluctuations in crop subsidies; the programs included in "Economic development, housing, and recreational and cultural activities" grew slightly between 1952 and 1972 but have since been stable. Finally, expenditures for the space program trace the manned moon voyage program.

**Support of the labor force.** Figure 2.20 shows trends for the four components of the "Support of the labor force" category.

*Support of the labor force primarily consists of Unemployment Insurance, which mirrors the cyclical nature of the economy.*

The major component in this subcategory is the mixed federal and state Unemployment Insurance program, whose most prominent feature is that it mirrors the cyclical performance of the economy and acts as a lubricant for the labor market by providing short-term financial assistance in instances of "frictional" unemployment. Moreover, it provides

---

[27]Appendix B presents a detailed listing of all components in this subcategory.

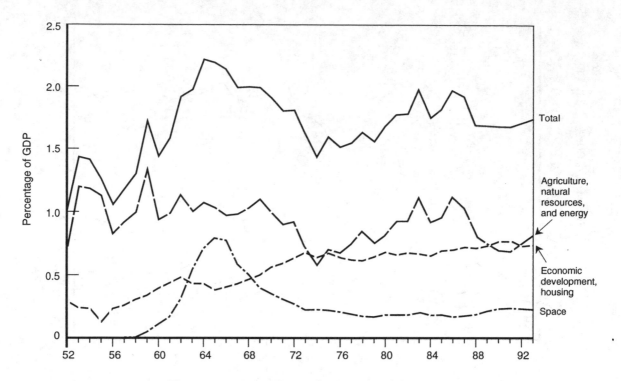

**Figure 2.19—Expenditures for Support of the Economy**

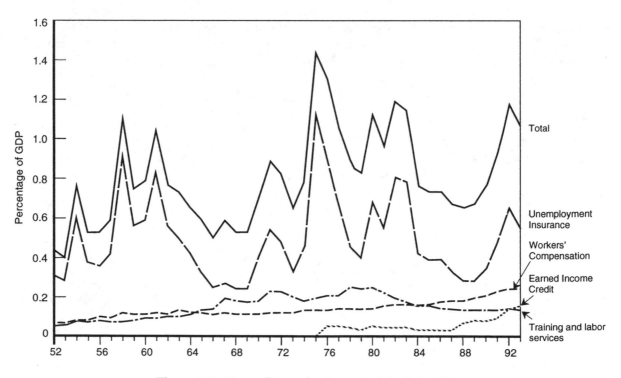

**Figure 2.20—Expenditures for Support of the Labor Force**

counterтercyclical transfer payments during recessions and thus is an automatic stabilizer.

The remaining components of the subcategory are small relative to Unemployment Insurance. "Training and labor services" consists of services performed for the labor force; the other two components are income-transfer programs. Workers' Compensation is a long-standing program conducted by both the federal and state governments. It has grown slowly and has recently become controversial because of alleged abuses. The Earned Income Credit program began in 1976 as a means of supplementing incomes of full-time workers whose incomes nonetheless left them in poverty. It is generally viewed as an alternative to welfare, since it offers an incentive to remain employed at whatever wage can be earned.

## Other Programs

The third category of domestic expenditures exists to house expenditures that otherwise would cloud trends in the "basic" and "support" categories (Figure 2.21). Utilities and commercial activities are, in most instances, government enterprises. NIPA records only surpluses or deficits resulting from current operations of these enterprises and treats

*The "Other programs" category is small and has not contributed to the growth in domestic expenditures.*

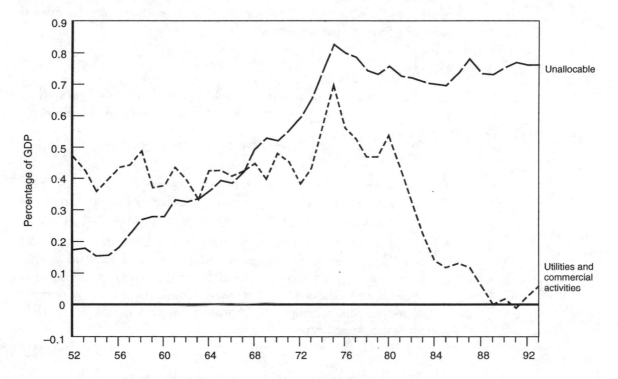

**Figure 2.21—Expenditures for Other Programs**

their physical investments in equipment and structures as government purchases.[28]

If these expenditures were included in their relevant functional areas of the "basic" or "support" categories, their declining deficits and small surpluses would tend to offset other government expenditures that are properly measured in the functional areas. For this reason, these expenditures have been collected here.

Since these enterprises receive subsidies, their financial position, as shown in Figure 2.21 but especially in the underlying detail in Appendix C, can be used to select promising candidates for privatization. Indeed, a portion of the decline relative to GDP in this category reflects elimination of Postal Service deficits, in the wake of the service becoming a quasi-private agency and thus increasingly subject to competition from private carriers. Rising lottery sales account for the remainder of the category's decline.

In general terms—and especially for local gas and electric utilities and water and sewer systems—surpluses from current operations have covered the major portion of investments. The level of these investments has been quite steady, in contrast with the volatility of investments in transportation infrastructure discussed earlier.

The second subcategory includes state and local expenditures that NIPA regards as "unallocable." This subcategory is small and mirrors overall trends in domestic public expenditures.

## SUMMARY

Our examination of the pattern of public expenditures over the past 41 years from a functional perspective has identified the following trends:

- Total public expenditures have grown by 6.8 percentage points of GDP.

- International expenditures, primarily defense expenditures, have been a declining share of the total, while domestic expenditures have swelled from about 10 percent to almost 25 percent of total GDP.

- The increase in domestic expenditures has been divided almost equally between basic programs (primarily education and health) and programs in support of individuals (primarily Social Security and welfare). The combined increase in basic programs and support of individuals accounts for almost 90 percent of the increase in domestic expenditures.

---

[28]For a detailed explanation of NIPA's treatment of government enterprises, see BEA (1988:6).

In the next chapter, we expand on these conclusions by examining total public expenditures from the analytic perspectives of the political jurisdictions undertaking the expenditures, the economic categories into which the expenditures fall, and the types of funds that finance the expenditures.

## 3. TRENDS IN U.S. TOTAL PUBLIC EXPENDITURES, 1952–1993, FROM THE PERSPECTIVES OF JURISDICTION, ECONOMIC TYPE, AND FUND

The functional classification of the preceding chapter tells us a good deal about the purposes behind public expenditures. Perspective on that question is gained by assuming that the United States has a single central fisc and general fund. In this chapter we relax this assumption and focus instead on the level of government that undertakes an expenditure; the type of fund that pays for the expenditure; and the economic character of the expenditure. These additional ways of classifying expenditures allow us to address four key questions:

- How have trends in total public expenditures differed across jurisdictions since 1952?

- How have the economic components of expenditures moved over this period?

- Which types of expenditure have seen more growth since 1952, regular budget or social insurance?

- Are there differences across jurisdictions in how regular budget and social insurance expenditures have behaved?

Taken together, the answers to these questions provide mutually reinforcing pictures of expenditures in the total public sector over the past 41 years. The first subsection pursues these questions for total public expenditures. The remainder of the chapter provides additional perspectives on federal and state and local expenditures, including some of their interrelationships.

### TOTAL PUBLIC EXPENDITURES

#### Overview

In Chapter 2 we noted that total public expenditures have grown by 6.8 percentage points of GDP since 1952. Using the analytic perspectives of this chapter, we can identify different patterns underlying this increase:

- By *jurisdiction*, the increase has occurred primarily in state and local public expenditures and only secondarily in federal public expenditures.

- By *type of expenditure*, the increase has occurred entirely in transfer payments and in net interest payments, partially offset by a decline in purchases of goods and services.

- By *fund*, most of the increase has occurred in the social insurance funds of the federal government and in the regular budget funds of the state and local governments, partially offset by a substantial decline in public expenditures from federal regular budget funds.

If we integrate these three perspectives, we see strong growth in federal social insurance budget transfer payments, state and local regular budget purchases and transfer payments, and federal regular budget net interest payments.

## Expenditures from the Perspective of Jurisdiction

Figures 3.1a and 3.1b summarize jurisdictional changes in total public expenditures between 1952 and 1993. Figure 3.1a shows aggregate federal "public," or nongrant, expenditures, as well as state and local expenditures; Figure 3.1b shows the magnitude of federal grants-in-aid to state and local governments relative to federal public expenditures and their total.

Because grants-in-aid are intergovernmental transfers of resources, rather than public expenditures, they differ qualitatively from federal public expenditures. Figure 3.1b shows grants and federal public expenditures on the same graph only to compare their relative magnitudes.[1]

*Federal public expenditures have stabilized at about 20 percent of GDP.*

After a 20-percent peak during the Korean War, federal public expenditures trended downward. Between 1955 and 1979, they fluctuated between 16 and 19 percent of GDP; they rose to 21 percent by 1983 and stabilized near that level.

*State and local expenditures have risen to more than a third of total public expenditures.*

A major trend of the past 41 years has been the substantial diffusion of public expenditures away from Washington and toward state and local governments and their subentities. State and local expenditures have increased dramatically, rising from 6.9 percent of GDP in 1952 to 13.0 percent in 1993.

Federal grants to state and local governments, which are included in this total, helped to fuel this expansion. These grants increased steadily through 1976, when they peaked at 3.5 percent of GDP. They remained at that level through 1978, before declining to 2.3 percent of GDP by 1989. More recently, grants have begun to rise again, reaching 2.9 percent of GDP in 1993.

## Expenditures from the Perspective of Economic Type

Figure 3.2 shows how the 6.8-percentage-point increase in total public expenditures between 1952 and 1993 was allocated across the economic categories of purchases, transfer payments, net interest payments, and subsidies less current surpluses of government enterprises (SGE). Overall, the expansion of total public expenditures over the past 41 years

---

[1]Additional explanation is contained in Appendix A as well as later in this chapter.

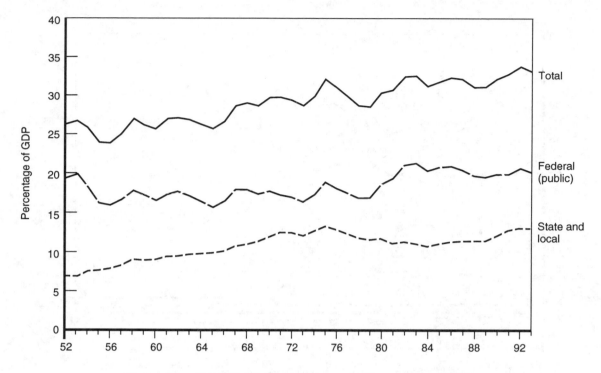

**Figure 3.1a—Total Public Expenditures as a Percentage of GDP**

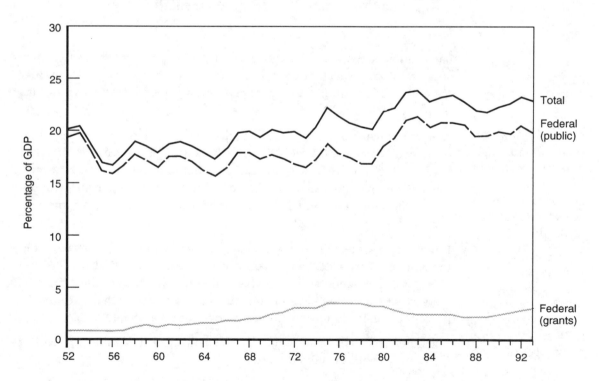

**Figure 3.1b—Total Federal Expenditures as a Percentage of GDP**

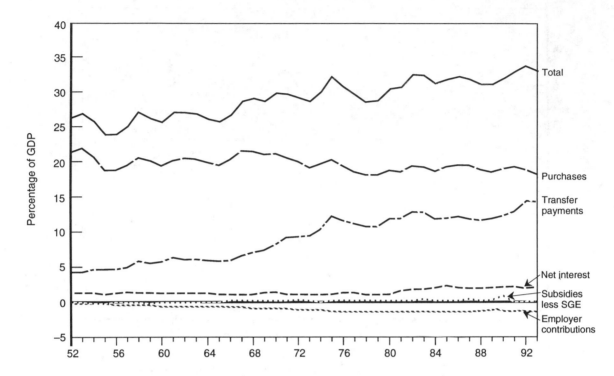

**Figure 3.2—Trends in Types of Public Expenditures**

has been episodic and strongly concentrated in payments to individuals and creditors. Meanwhile, the value of purchases used to conduct government programs that produce public goods and services has declined relative to GDP.

*All of the relative growth in expenditures has occurred in two economic categories—transfers and net interest payments.*

Transfer payments have nearly quadrupled in relative terms, moving from 4 to 14 percent of GDP. The bulk of this increase took place between 1965 and 1975, with the category holding roughly constant relative to GDP over the balance of the period until a very recent surge in the 1990s. Between 1979 and 1984, net interest payments doubled, moving from 1 to 2 percent of GDP.

*Purchases of goods and services by all levels of government have been basically stable at 20 percent of GDP over the entire 41-year period.*

Purchases have peaked twice at nearly 22 percent of GDP—once during the Korean War in 1953 and again during the Vietnam War in 1967 and 1968, when nondefense purchases also were growing rapidly. Otherwise, purchases have fluctuated in a very narrow band around 20 percent of GDP and have remained below this level since 1975.

Subsidies less SGE have remained constant at an insignificant level of GDP throughout the period.[2]

_____

[2]As explained in Chapter 1, however, only residual surpluses or deficits of government enterprises constitute payments between government and nongovernment

Finally, recall from the discussion of government retirement in Chapter 2 that government employer contributions to their employees' trust funds are an interfund transaction. Therefore, we deduct these contributions to arrive at "net" retirement and thereby avoid double-counting within public expenditure totals. Similar deductions are required in this chapter to maintain the same definition and total for public expenditures. We have made these deductions by jurisdiction in the calculations for Figure 3.1a, and the deductions appear as negative values in Figures 3.2 and 3.3, labeled "Employer contributions." Government employer retirement contributions have increased steadily from 0.4 percent of GDP in 1952 to 1.3 percent in 1993. For further explanation of these interfund transactions, see Appendix A.

### Expenditures from the Perspective of Type of Fund

Figure 3.3 shows total public expenditures by their funding source—regular versus social insurance.

Regular budget expenditures accounted for roughly 25 percent of GDP in 1952–1953 (during the Korean War) and between 1967 and 1975 (during the Vietnam War through the recession of 1974–1975). At other times they fluctuated around 23 percent of GDP, with occasional dips to or below 22 percent. However, a surge since 1980 brought regular budget public expenditures of all jurisdictions to 27.7 percent of GDP in 1993.

Leaving aside cyclical effects, social insurance expenditures rose rapidly through the mid-1970s, grew more slowly until the early 1980s, and were roughly steady for the balance of the period.[3] This growth over the past four decades dominates the fund-based perspective on total public expenditures.

Finally, government employer retirement contributions increased steadily from 0.4 percent of GDP in 1952 to 1.3 percent in 1993. These contributions are intragovernmental transactions rather than public expenditures; they are shown in Figure 3.3 only to indicate their magnitude relative to overall social insurance expenditures.

*For most of the period, regular budget public expenditures fluctuated between 23 and 25 percent of GDP, but they have risen recently to nearly 28 percent.*

*Social insurance expenditures increased from 1.5 percent of GDP in 1952 to almost 7 percent in 1993.*

---

sectors of the economy and thus qualify as public expenditures. Hence, Figure 3.2 does not reflect fully the enterprises' activities in the economy. For example, only the residual surplus or deficit of Postal Service operations contributes to the figure, even though the Service is a huge employer and purchaser. For an explanation of how NIPA treats government enterprises, see BEA (1988:6).

[3]Because social insurance expenditures contain both Unemployment Insurance and Social Security benefits, they are more sensitive to business-cycle fluctuations than other categories of expenditures. Hence, the peaks shown for the category in 1958, 1975, and 1982 reflect recession-induced drops in GDP for those years, as well as increases in absolute social insurance expenditures and other noncyclical effects.

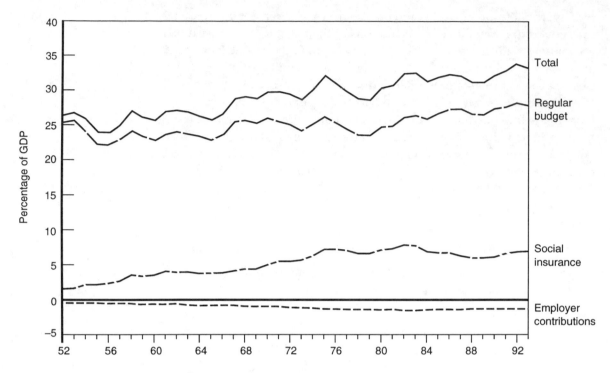

**Figure 3.3—Funding Sources for Total Public Expenditures**

## Differences Across Jurisdictions in Regular Budget and Social Insurance Expenditure Trends

Figure 3.4a shows how the jurisdictional allocation of regular budget expenditures has changed over time. Federal public expenditures and grants are shown separately in Figure 3.4b.

*State and local regular budget expenditures have risen steadily and now constitute nearly half of the total regular budget.*

One of the most important trends in public expenditures since 1952 has been the shift in regular budgets from federal dominance to a nearly equal split with the state and local governments. Federal regular budget public expenditures have fallen relative to the economy—moving from 18.3 percent of GDP in 1952 to 14.1 percent in 1993. Much of this reduction has been reallocated to state and local governments through grants. However, federal grants have provided resources for only a portion of the state and local expansion.

The state and local expansion has been nearly continuous throughout the period. The state and local share of regular budget public expenditures has grown from just over a quarter in 1952 to almost half in 1993. These expenditures have nearly doubled relative to the economy—moving from 7.0 percent of GDP in 1952 to 13.6 percent in 1993. In the 1970s, state and local expenditures actually exceeded federal public expenditures.

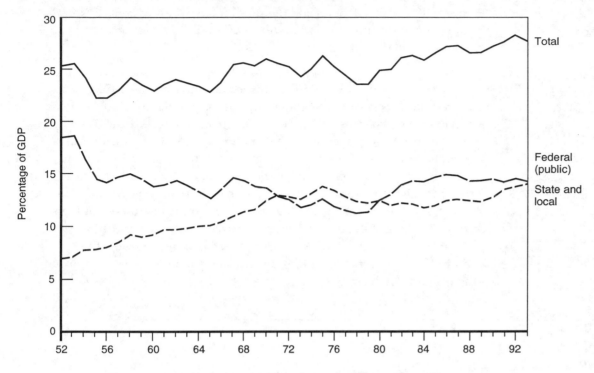

**Figure 3.4a—Jurisdictional Share of Regular Budget Expenditures**

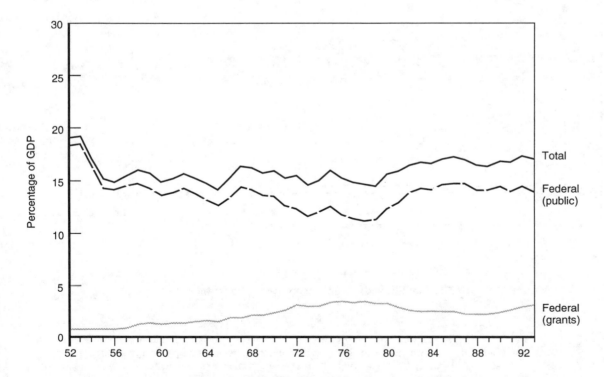

**Figure 3.4b—Federal Grants Relative to Federal Regular Budget Public Expenditures**

52

*All of the growth in aggregate social insurance expenditures relative to GDP has occurred at the federal level.*

Figure. 3.5 shows the federal and the state and local components of social insurance expenditures. The growth in expenditures has been entirely concentrated at the federal level.

Two additional features of Figure 3.5 merit comment. First, *net* state and local social insurance expenditures turned negative in the 1980s. This occurred both because of the way state and local social insurance funds are managed and because of the way NIPA treats interest earnings. State and local social insurance funds consist almost entirely of pension funds for public employees. Generally, these funds have sought to provide current retirement benefits while building reserves by accumulating interest and dividend earnings from investments in various financial instruments. Within aggregate state and local social insurance budgets during the 1980s, these earnings from reserves exceeded current transfer payments. In general, NIPA treats interest earnings as negative expenditures.[4] Consequently, the aggregate state and local social insurance fund expenditures during the 1980s are negative.

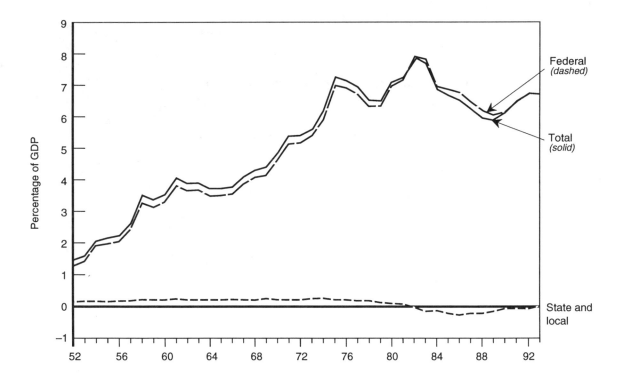

**Figure 3.5—Jurisdictional Share of Social Insurance Expenditures**

---

[4]NIPA actually treats interest earnings inconsistently among its tables—as deductions from interest payments (i.e., negative expenditures) in its major tables for the government sector (301, 302, and 303), as receipts in its specialized table for social insurance funds (314), and as a deduction from transfer payments in its state and local functional table (317). To reconcile these tables in Chapters 2 and 3, we have consistently treated interest earnings as negative expenditures. For further explanation, see Appendix A.

Second, Unemployment Insurance is the only major category of social insurance that the federal and state jurisdictions manage jointly.[5] Although states set their own contribution and benefit levels for much of this program, the federal government directly pays some beneficiaries, loans money to state funds that are temporarily exhausted, and extends benefit periods temporarily during recessions. Disbursements from this fund are negatively correlated with GDP and hence generate peaks in Figure 3.5 that accompany recessions, like those that occurred in 1958, 1961, 1975, and 1982.

## PERSPECTIVES ON FEDERAL EXPENDITURES

We have identified two major trends in public expenditures over the past 41 years—the growth in federal social insurance expenditures, and the jurisdictional shift toward state and local expenditures in regular budgets. In this subsection, we will examine the federal role in these trends. We first examine federal expenditures in the aggregate, then discuss regular budget and social insurance expenditures separately. The aggregate view usually receives the most attention in discussions of federal expenditures.[6] However, separate treatment of federal regular and social insurance budgets clarifies the federal role in the two major national public expenditure trends.

### Overview

Since 1952 defense purchases have declined relative to GDP in the federal regular budget, while grants to state and local governments and net interest payments have increased. Taken together, the drop in defense and the rise in net interest payments and grants have approximately canceled each other out and left federal regular budget expenditures roughly constant relative to GDP. Over the same period, federal social insurance expenditures have risen very rapidly because Social Security transfer payments increased, as did the Hospital Insurance component of Medicare after 1965. Since the federal regular budget has remained roughly constant relative to GDP, the increase in the federal social insurance budget roughly corresponds to the increase in total federal expenditures since 1952.

*The increase in federal social insurance expenditures accounts for all growth in aggregate federal expenditures since 1952.*

---

[5]Rather than split the funds by jurisdiction, both NIPA and this report include Unemployment Insurance entirely in the federal social insurance budget.

[6]Indeed, if loans and certain other financial activities are ignored, a NIPA-defined aggregate federal budget roughly approximates the federal unified budget. For a reconciliation of the aggregate federal account in NIPA and the unified budget, see BEA (1992–1993: Table 318B).

## A Breakdown of Total Federal Expenditures by Fund

Figure 3.6 shows the increase in total federal expenditures by type of fund—regular and social insurance, including government employer retirement contributions. Following the Korean War, federal regular budget expenditures moved in a narrow band between 14.2 and 16.4 percent of GDP until 1979. Then, in the 1980s, these expenditures began to grow and ranged between 15.7 and 17.5 percent through 1993. Since 1952, federal social insurance expenditures have increased from 1.3 to 6.7 percent of GDP.

If the peak during the Korean War is excluded, federal expenditures have grown by roughly 7 percentage points of GDP since 1955. This increase is made up of a 5-point increase in social insurance expenditures through 1975 and a 2.5-point increase in regular budget expenditures since just 1979.

To examine this long-term trend in more detail, we will consider regular budget and social insurance expenditures separately.

**Federal regular budget expenditures.** To understand trends in federal regular budget expenditures over the past 41 years, it is useful to separate regular budget purchases into their defense and nondefense components, leaving other economic categories of expenditures unchanged. Figures 3.7a and 3.7b show this categorization of expenditures since 1952.

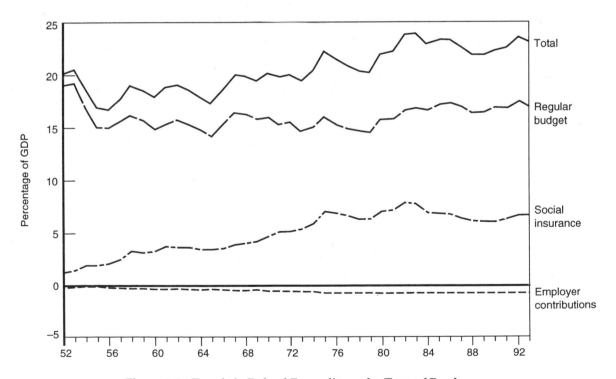

Figure 3.6—Trends in Federal Expenditures by Type of Fund

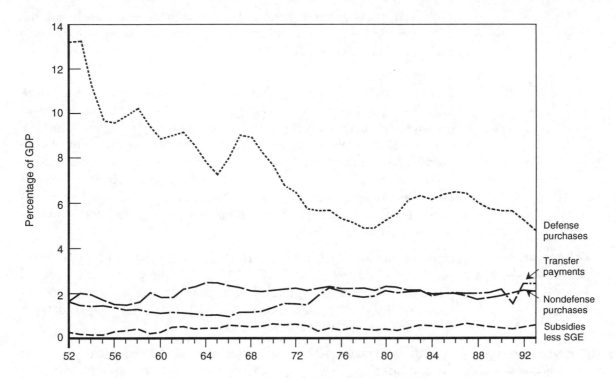

**Figure 3.7a—Defense and Nondefense Components of Federal Regular Budget Expenditures**

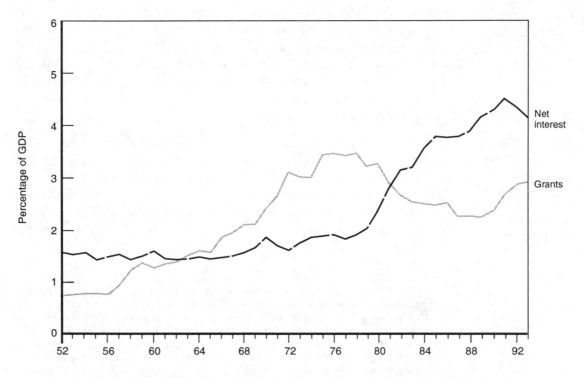

**Figure 3.7b—Federal Regular Budget Expenditures on Interest and Grants**

The clear message of Figures 3.7a and 3.7b is that nearly all the movement in the federal regular budget has been in defense purchases, grants, and net interest payments.

The three remaining expenditure categories, shown along the bottom of Figure 3.7a, can be combined and called "nondefense program expenditures," a useful composite category. It has fluctuated narrowly and grown slowly over the entire period because the federal government has not played the major *direct* role in most domestic regular budget programs. Rather, state and local governments have provided the bulk of domestic public services: education, transportation, police and corrections, and so on. In effect, the federal government has contracted out portions of its domestic program initiatives to state and local governments through grants-in-aid.

*Defense purchases have fallen relative to GDP.*

Defense purchases fell dramatically over the period. In 1956, defense purchases stood at 9.6 percent of GDP. By 1993, they had dropped to 4.8 percent, or by almost 5 percentage points, despite showing substantial volatility during the Vietnam War and the Carter-Reagan defense buildup of the late 1970s and early 1980s.

*The drop in defense expenditures has been offset by federal grants, and especially by a dramatic increase in interest payments.*

As defense purchases have fallen relative to GDP, federal regular budget expenditures on domestic programs have increased, mainly indirectly through grants to state and local government.[7]

However, grants have offset only a portion of the decline in defense purchases. The balance has been taken up by the dramatic increase of net interest payments in the federal regular budget since 1979. These payments rose because large federal regular budget deficits occurred while real interest rates were high in the early and mid-1980s. Net interest payments have exceeded grants since 1981. Moreover, in 1992 they amounted to 80 percent of nondefense program expenditures or 87 percent of defense expenditures.

*Excluding interest payments, federal regular budget expenditures have fallen as a percentage of GDP since 1952.*

Figure 3.8 summarizes these trends. Total programmatic (i.e., non–interest payment) federal regular budget expenditures—defense and nondefense purchases, transfers, subsidies less SGE, and grants—have declined slowly but steadily relative to GDP. Despite some variation, partially reflecting cyclical variation, the long-term trend in all program expenditures has been gently downward-sloping relative to the economy.

---

[7]The full story is slightly more complex. During the 1950s, the Interstate Highway program provided the first impetus to growth in grants. Between 1967 and 1978, from the peak of defense expenditures during the Vietnam War at 9.0 percent of GDP to their low point before the Carter-Reagan buildup at 4.9 percent, about 40 percent of the decline in defense spending was reallocated to increase grants. During this period, grants moved from 2.0 to 3.5 percent of GDP. In the course of the defense buildup during the early 1980s, grants fell back to 2.3 percent of GDP but have risen again more recently with post–Cold War reductions in defense spending.

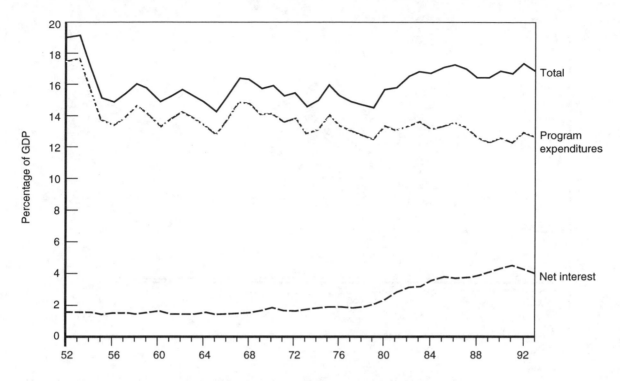

**Figure 3.8—Federal Budget Expenditures, Excluding Net Interest**

**Federal social insurance expenditures.** In contrast to the relatively stable trend for total federal regular budget expenditures over 41 years, the pattern for federal social insurance expenditures is dynamic, as Figure 3.9a shows. The transfer-payment component of these expenditures is by far the largest and has grown from 1.5 percent of GDP to 7.8 percent. Since this growth is measured relative to GDP, social insurance transfer payments have grown much more rapidly than the economy as a whole, gaining an additional percentage point of GDP about every six years. As Figure 3.9b indicates, most of the growth in federal transfer payments has taken place in only two social insurance programs: Social Security and the Hospital Insurance (HI) component of Medicare.[8] These two programs alone grew from 0.6 percent of GDP in 1952 to 6.1 percent in 1993, a tenfold increase.

In addition to this dramatic increase in federal social insurance transfers, net interest *receipts* on social insurance fund balances, displayed as negative expenditures, have also grown, as shown in Figure 3.9a. These funds are managed differently from regular budget funds. Because the

*Federal social insurance transfer payments have surged, growing by 1 percentage point of GDP every six years. Most of the expansion has occurred in Social Security and in Medicare.*

---

[8]As Appendix A explains, the Supplemental Medical Insurance component of Medicare is included in the federal regular budget, where it has been the only major direct domestic program that has experienced rapid growth in recent years.

58

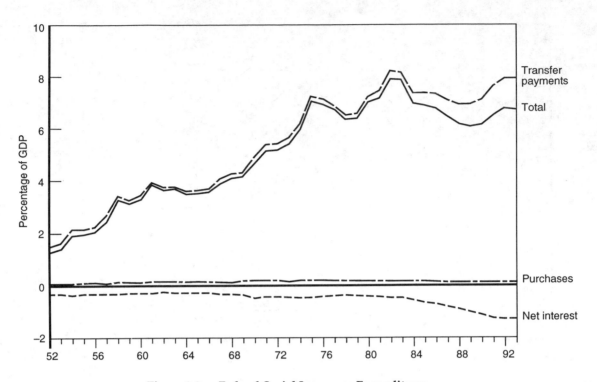

**Figure 3.9a—Federal Social Insurance Expenditures**

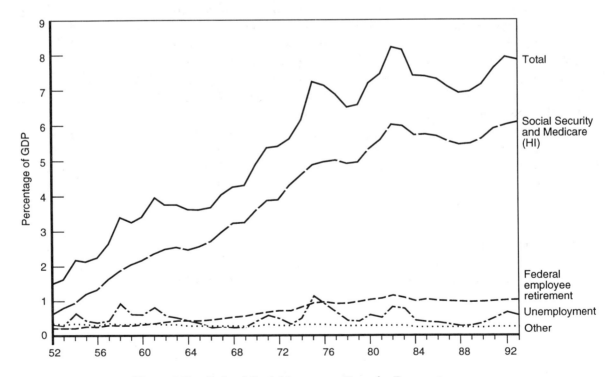

**Figure 3.9b—Federal Social Insurance Transfer Payments**

government acts as a trustee for current and eventual beneficiaries, the individual funds maintain reserves.  These reserves earn interest that builds the funds and strengthens their long-term financing.  Thus, the high interest rates of the early 1980s had an effect on the federal social insurance budget opposite to their effect on the federal regular budget. While high interest rates drove up the costs of federal borrowing in the regular budget, they also increased interest earnings on government debt held as assets by the various social insurance funds.

The administrative (purchase) expenses of operating the federal social insurance funds have been steady and small relative to GDP over the entire period.  The overhead expenses associated with these funds have not increased in proportion to the growth in their transfer payments.

## PERSPECTIVES ON STATE AND LOCAL PUBLIC EXPENDITURES

"State and local public expenditures" is a category that reflects statistical convenience, rather than political reality, since it represents activities of all state and local government entities acting, in large measure, without mutual knowledge or coordination.  The figures in this subsection are composites that represent a vast array of state and local governments. This is a simplifying assumption that gives rise to an interesting sort of aggregation paradox, due to the differences that do exist in expenditures among specific localities.  For example, a resident of California could be considerably more affected by expenditures on, say, earthquake-resistant school buildings than might a resident of Iowa.  Indeed, it is worth noting that no resident need live in the world represented by the aggregates—hence, the paradox.

### Overview

From this composite view emerge trends that complement the trends in federal expenditures.  For example, total state and local expenditures increased by 6 percentage points of GDP between 1952 and 1993 and in the process offset the decline in federal defense expenditures in the aggregate regular budget.

*The increase in state and local expenditures since 1952 has offset the decline in federal defense expenditures.*

Because *direct* federal regular budget expenditures for domestic programs have grown slowly and erratically, most of the increase in total domestic public expenditures has been concentrated at the state and local levels of government, the main providers of domestic public services. The major federal role in this domestic expansion has been through indirect expenditures, or grants-in-aid, which have financed a portion of the state and local expansion, albeit with great fluctuations.

*State and local expenditures account for most of the increase in domestic expenditures.*

Most of the domestic program growth occurred in purchases between 1952 and 1975, in response to demographically driven demands discussed in Chapter 2.  The other large contributor has been expansion of regular budget transfer payments during two periods: the increase related to the Great Society program in 1966–1972, and the recent rise beginning in 1990. In contrast to the federal regular budget, net interest payments have not played a major role at the state and local level.

### Total State and Local Expenditures

*Purchases and transfers have shaped state and local expenditures.*

Figure 3.10 categorizes total state and local public expenditures by their economic type. Purchases dominate the 41-year trend, in terms of both magnitude and growth. Transfer payments exhibit stair-step growth between 1966 and 1972 and again between 1989 and 1993. Expenditures for both net interest payments and subsidies less SGE are generally negative, and state and local government employer contributions to their employees' retirement trust funds are also shown as negative expenditures.

### State and Local Regular Budget Expenditures

Figure 3.11a is the analog of Figure 3.10 for state and local regular budget expenditures. Between 1952 and 1975, these expenditures doubled in aggregate, moving from 7 to nearly 14 percent of GDP. Over the succeeding three years, they declined to 12 percent of GDP and remained at that level until 1989, after which they rose sharply.

The long expansion in these expenditures between 1952 and 1975 was concentrated, for the most part, in purchases and occurred largely be-

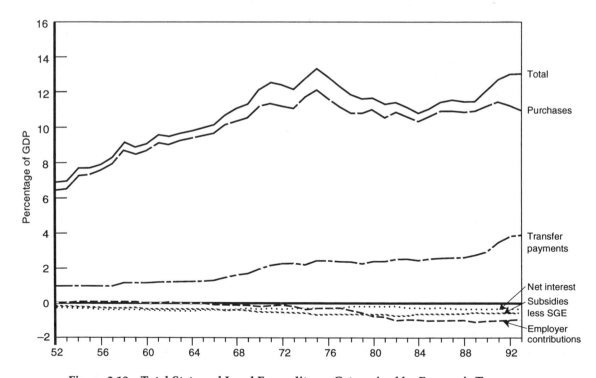

**Figure 3.10—Total State and Local Expenditures Categorized by Economic Type**

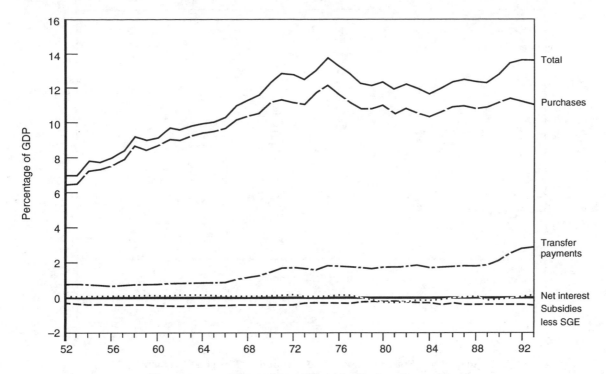

**Figure 3.11a—State and Local Regular Budget Expenditures**

cause of demands placed upon public services by the post–World War II baby boom. Thus, as we noted in Chapter 2, much of this expansion was fueled by increased spending on public education and police. The Great Society program also contributed to this expansion by increasing regular budget transfer payments between 1966 and 1972; these transfer payments doubled as a percentage of GDP between 1966 and 1975.

After 1975, the expansion in purchases associated with the baby boom ended, and overall expenditures on transfer programs stabilized as continued growth in state and local medical care (Figure 2.12) was offset by slowdowns in welfare income-support programs (Figure 2.18). Taken together, these factors spelled the end of increases in state and local regular budget expenditures relative to the economy, and through the 1980s these expenditures grew at roughly the same rate as GDP. In 1990, they began to rise again, primarily because of increased transfers associated with state components of Medicaid and welfare assistance.

In sharp contrast to their explosive growth at the federal level, net interest payments at state and local levels of government, shown with a magnified scale in Figure 3.11b, have been small relative to GDP. Since these governments have generally maintained cash balances in current accounts and raised money through bond sales that have not been expended immediately, their interest earnings have offset interest payments. These governments have also tended to maintain interest-

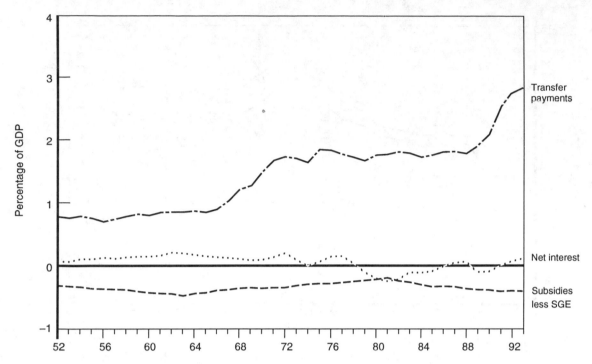

**Figure 3.11b—State and Local Transfer and Net Interest Payments**

earning reserves due to constitutional requirements for balanced general-fund budgets.[9]

Surpluses from current operations of state and local government enterprises have tended to exceed their very small subsidies, thus sending the difference negative.[10]  In general, municipal utilities such as water, sewerage, gas, and electricity have generated surpluses, as have toll roads, airports, liquor stores, and publicly sponsored lotteries and off-track betting.  Public transit operations have been the major source of deficits.

### How State and Local Governments Use Federal Grants

*State and local governments view federal grants as receipts and may use them to finance a variety of regular budget expenditures.*

The earlier discussion of the federal regular budget suggests that despite their volatility, grants have been the major vehicle for federal domestic initiatives.  It is frequently assumed that a federal grant causes additional state and local expenditures and that these expenditures occur in the program, or for the purpose, that the grant specifies.  Neither part of this assumption need hold in a specific instance, however, since grants are fungible against state and local funds in the jurisdictions' regular budgets.

---

[9]It is important to note, however, that the time path of interest payments within a specific jurisdiction may be quite different from this composite picture.

[10] These surpluses represent only results of the enterprises' current operations, since their capital investments are included in purchases.

On the one hand, grants may indeed finance a new program or increase expenditures on an existing program. On the other, however, grants may displace state or local funds: While a grant maintains an existing level of expenditure for a targeted program, state and local funds may be reallocated to another program, one that may be different from the program or purpose that the grant specifies. In the extreme case, a grant may fully replace state and local funds that are diverted to reduce a deficit or finance a tax cut, while expenditures again remain constant.[11]

We can gain some perspective on the role of grants in state and local expenditures by comparing state and local regular budget expenditures with the magnitude of federal grants, on the assumption that the grants actually finance expenditures. The difference between grants and total regular budget expenditures then represents expenditures financed by sources other than grants.

Figure 3.12 reproduces the trend in state and local regular budget expenditures from Figure 3.11a and shows the trend in federal grants. In addition, Figure 3.12 shows the difference between expenditures and grants, which represents the level of expenditures that state and local governments funded from sources other than grants.

These data indicate that despite their episodic character, grants have played a major role in financing state and local regular budget expenditures. In addition, however, the episodic character of grants has made them a lagging source of finance, a characteristic with important implications for the conduct of government at the state and local levels.

*Grants have been a lagging source of income for state and local governments.*

State and local regular budget expenditures have seen five epochs:

- 1952–1971: A long, steady increase that was mainly driven by the demographics of the baby boom;

- 1971–1975: The final increase, partly reflecting a drop in GDP during the 1974–1975 recession;

---

[11]For an excellent study of state grantsmanship and fungibility, see Derthick (1975). Between 1972 and 1987, general revenue-sharing made grants that augmented their recipients' financial resources without directing or requiring their subsequent expenditure. In essence, funds obtained under this program were fungible upon receipt.

Other grants-in-aid frequently have included conditions on the use of funds received, and these conditions may indeed restrict fungibility. In addition to the self-explanatory conditions of aid (COA), the federal government has also imposed legal or administrative direct orders (DOs), which are unrelated to aid it provides. Both COAs and DOs are subsumed under the less formal term "mandates," with the expression "unfunded mandates" applied to mandates that are unaccompanied by financing.

Although federal mandates were almost nonexistent during the 1950s, they were put in place more frequently during the 1960s and have grown rapidly in recent years. In addition, the situation for local governments is compounded, since these governments receive financial transfers from their states, and these transfers are frequently accompanied by COAs and DOs far more numerous than the federal restrictions. Additional, though rather dated, discussion is contained in Lovell and Tobin (1981:318).

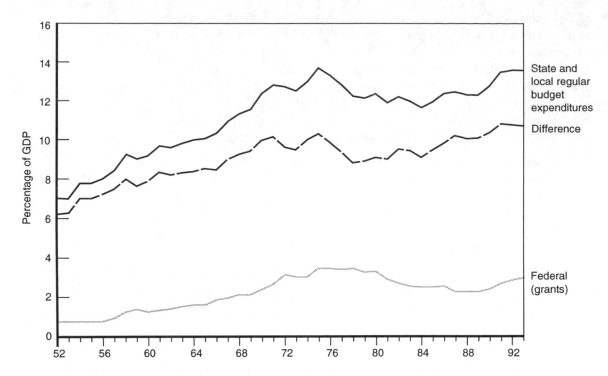

**Figure 3.12—Trends in State and Local Regular Budget Expenditures and in Federal Grants**

- 1975–1978: A sharp decline, following the crest of the baby-boom–induced demand for services;

- 1978–1989: A long period of constancy relative to the economy; and

- 1990–1993: The sharp rise in recent years.

Detailed data for the five epochs are shown in Table 3.1 and discussed below.

- First, federal grants financed about a third of the increase in state and local regular budget expenditures through 1971, or 1.9 percentage points of GDP compared with a total expenditure increase of 5.8 percentage points. The remaining two-thirds of the expenditure increase was funded by state and local resources.

- Second, the heyday of federal revenue-sharing occurred between 1972 (the year of the program's inception) and 1978. Between 1971 and 1975, federal grants increased by 0.8 percentage point of GDP and expenditures increased by 0.9 point; thus, grants fueled nearly all of the final increase in state and local expenditures during this period.

- Third, with recovery from the recession of 1974–1975 and reduced demographic pressures, state and local expenditures dropped relative to the economy between 1975 and 1978, declining by 1.4 percentage points of GDP. Federal grants remained steady during this

Table 3.1

STATE AND LOCAL REGULAR BUDGET EXPENDITURES AND FEDERAL
GRANTS: 1952–1992

| | 1952 | 1971 | 1975 | 1978 | 1989 | 1992 |
|---|---|---|---|---|---|---|
| | Percentage of GDP | | | | | |
| Expenditures | 7.0 | 12.8 | 13.7 | 12.3 | 12.3 | 13.6 |
| Grants | 0.7 | 2.6 | 3.4 | 3.5 | 2.3 | 2.9 |
| Difference | 6.2 | 10.1 | 10.3 | 8.8 | 10.1 | 10.7 |
| | Change in Percentage Points of GDP | | | | | |
| | 1952–1971 | 1971–1975 | 1975–1978 | 1978–1989 | 1989–1992 | |
| Expenditures | 5.8 | 0.9 | −1.4 | 0.0 | 1.3 | |
| Grants | 1.9 | 0.8 | 0.0 | −1.2 | 0.6 | |
| Difference | 3.9 | 0.1 | −1.4 | 1.3 | 0.6 | |

NOTE: Columns may not sum due to rounding.

period, however, and state and local governments hence captured the reduction in expenditures—in the form of relief upon their own resources.

- Fourth, while state and local expenditures were constant relative to GDP between 1978 and 1989, federal grants declined by 1.2 percentage points of GDP. The reductions affected both categorical grants and revenue-sharing, which terminated in 1987. As a result, state and local financing requirements steadily rose with no increase in aggregate services to show for the rise.

- Finally, the sharp rise in state and local expenditures beginning in 1990 was accompanied by a mild recession as well as program expansions. During this epoch, most of the growth in grants was in the Medicaid program. All told, state and local expenditures increased by 1.3 percentage points of GDP; federal grants financed 0.6 point, or nearly half, of this rapid expansion.

At different times grants have supported, stimulated, and restrained aggregate growth in state and local expenditures. Moreover, from the viewpoint of the recipients, the magnitude of grants has been unpredictable. Grants provided windfalls in the late 1970s, a time of state and local tax reduction. In contrast, reductions in grants during the 1980s forced state and local governments to search for alternative sources of finance. As a result of this volatility, state and local receipts from sources other than grants have displayed more variation than aggregate state and local expenditures, and grants have been a source of instability in state and local budgets.

*Grants have also caused instability in state and local revenues.*

## State and Local Social Insurance Expenditures

Figure 3.13 shows the economic components of state and local social insurance expenditures. As mentioned previously, the state and local

66

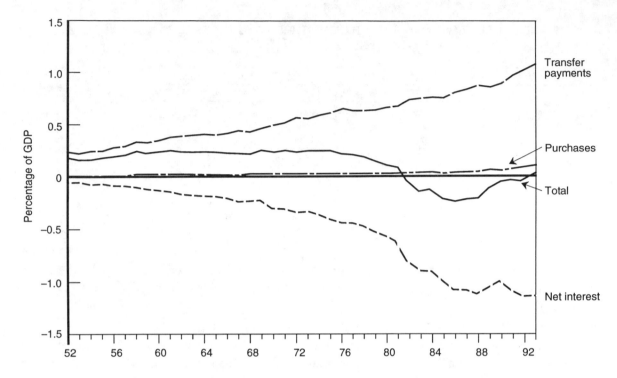

**Figure 3.13—State and Local Social Insurance Expenditures**

social insurance funds are devoted almost entirely to retirement accounts for public employees; there are also small funds for temporary disability and workers' compensation benefits.

*Interest earnings have offset state and local social insurance expenditures.*

Between 1952 and 1978, state and local social insurance transfer payments rose from 0.2 percent of GDP to 0.6 percent, but interest earnings, shown as negative expenditures in Figure 3.13, offset the increase. Consequently, net expenditures remained steady at 0.2 percent of GDP. Contributions from both employers and employees built large reserves that were invested in various financial instruments during this period. After 1978, high real interest rates, operating on these reserves, led to higher earnings and sent net total expenditures negative. Recently, the net total has moved toward neutrality.

## SUMMARY

When we view total expenditures from the perspectives of jurisdiction, economic category, and type of fund, we see two major trends: the growth in federal social insurance expenditures, and the shift toward state and local jurisdictions in regular budgets. Some of the most important details underlying these trends are listed below.

- Total public spending rose by 6.8 percentage points of GDP between 1951 and 1993. Federal public expenditures were roughly 20 percent of GDP throughout that period, but state and local expenditures grew dramatically and now constitute more than a third of total public expenditures.

- All of the relative growth in total public expenditures has occurred in transfer payments to individuals and in net interest payments on the federal debt.

- Federal expenditures no longer dominate the regular budget: The state and local share is now nearly 50 percent.

- All of the growth in social insurance expenditures occurred at the federal level. Indeed, the increase in federal social insurance expenditures accounts for all growth in total federal expenditures since 1952. Most of this growth has taken place in just two programs: Social Security and the Hospital Insurance portion of Medicare.

- In the federal regular budget, defense expenditures have fallen relative to GDP, but the drop has been offset by increased federal grants, and especially by a dramatic increase in interest payments. If interest payments are excluded, federal regular budget expenditures have fallen as a percentage of GDP over the past 41 years.

- Purchases have driven the growth of total state and local expenditures since 1952. Purchases and transfer payments dominate the regular budget, but earnings from interest have offset social insurance expenditures. State and local governments have used federal grants to finance some regular budget expenditures, but grants have lagged and have been a source of instability in state and local financing.

# 4. CONCLUSIONS

In this chapter we summarize the trends in public expenditures discussed in the preceding chapters and draw their policy implications.

## AN ANALYTIC REVIEW

### The Functions of Public Expenditures

As public expenditures have grown relative to the economy over the past 41 years, a major change has occurred in how they are allocated across the functions of government. As Table 4.1 shows, a relatively small number of major categories have participated in this growth and reallocation.

Total public expenditures have risen by 6.8 percentage points of GDP since 1952. This increase is the net result of striking reductions in one group of categories and increases in another.

Expenditures on defense and veterans' benefits have fallen by more than 9 percentage points, mostly because the relative burden of defense

*Growth in public expenditures since 1952 is the result of lower defense and higher domestic expenditures relative to the economy.*

Table 4.1

CHANGES IN FUNCTIONAL CATEGORIES OF PUBLIC EXPENDITURES

| | Percentage of GDP | | |
| --- | --- | --- | --- |
| | 1952 | 1993 | Difference |
| **Total public expenditures** | **26.3** | **33.1** | **+6.8** |
| National defense | 13.2 | 4.8 | −8.4 |
| Veterans' compensation[a] | 1.1 | 0.3 | −0.8 |
| Social Security | 0.6 | 4.7 | +4.1 |
| Medicare | 0.0 | 2.4 | +2.4 |
| State and local medical care[b] | 0.0 | 2.1 | +2.1 |
| Welfare and social services | 0.4 | 1.4 | +1.0 |
| Primary and secondary education | 2.0 | 3.9 | +1.9 |
| Higher education | 0.3 | 1.0 | +0.7 |
| Police and corrections | 0.4 | 1.2 | +0.8 |
| Net government employee retirement | −0.1 | 0.6 | +0.7 |
| Net interest payments | 1.3 | 1.9 | +0.6 |
| Unallocable (state and local) | 0.2 | 0.8 | +0.6 |
| General government activities | 0.9 | 1.2 | +0.3 |
| Residual[c] | 6.0 | 6.8 | +0.8 |

[a]Excludes education and health benefits.
[b]Includes federal Medicaid grants.
[c]Each category in the residual changed by less than 0.3 percentage point of GDP in absolute value. The residual includes rounding error.

expenditures has decreased as the economy has grown. In addition, however, the past 41 years have seen a redefinition of the U.S. role in world affairs that has both contributed to the overall relative decline in international expenditures and reversed the overall trend during several periods of time. For example, the era of Marshall Plan foreign economic assistance gave way to vigorous economic competition from former aid recipients, even if political competition has remained somewhat more muted. Likewise, a war and multiple confrontations with Soviet client states—as well as the potential for more of each—drove defense expenditures upward over several periods relative to the overall downward trend during the period. Finally, the Vietnam mobilization followed on the heels of the first strategic-force acquisition program.

With the end of the Cold War, the expectation is that defense expenditures will decrease further. Whether this expectation will be borne out or a new regime of collective security will be necessary in the remarkably disorderly post–Cold War "new world order" remains to be seen, as does the U.S. role in that order.

*Five categories account for most of the increase in expenditures: Social Security, medical care, welfare and social services, education, and police and corrections.*

While this decline was taking place, all other expenditures increased by 16 percentage points of GDP. Only five expenditure categories accounted for 13 points of this increase—Social Security, medical care, welfare and social services, public education, and police and corrections. All other expenditure categories—space, agricultural subsidies, and the other categories that so frequently seem to dominate public debate—competed for the remaining 3 percentage points of GDP, and net interest payments made up one-fifth of this residual amount.

The four expenditure categories showing the most growth had definite beneficiary groups within the U.S. population: the elderly (Social Security and Medicare), the poor (medical, welfare, and social services), and the young (education). The increase in the fifth expenditure category—police and corrections—was targeted against the criminal.

In addition, at least to a first order, a small number of factors account for these increases. The successive cohorts of the post–World War II baby boom largely shaped expenditures for public primary and secondary education after 1952, and these expenditures, in turn, dominated education expenditures as a whole. Likewise, subsequent encounters of these cohorts with the law-enforcement and criminal-justice systems, and especially policy decisions leading to tougher sentencing, drove police and corrections expenditures.

Meanwhile, at the other end of the age distribution, both the pool of those eligible for Social Security benefits and the magnitude of these benefits increased rapidly over the period. These programmatic changes, and to a lesser extent the increased proportion of elderly in the population, have resulted in the growth shown in Table 4.1. Medicare expenditures, too, increased because of the larger proportion of elderly in the population, but the more important factor in their increase has been the increasing costs of medical care delivery, which some reliable analysts have attributed to enhancements in medical technology. State and local medical expenditures, including federal Medicaid grants, have likewise increased as medical costs have risen.

Finally, it is worth noting in passing that although the increased proportion of elderly in the U.S. population has contributed to the growth of Social Security and Medicare expenditures, it does not seem to have been the prime cause of these categories' increase. However, as the baby-boom cohorts that drove education and police expenditures age, the increased proportion of elderly will take on a more prominent role in shaping these expenditures than has been true in the past.

These five expenditure categories, then, and the underlying sources of their movement merit the attention of those interested in the growth of government expenditures and their potential for being controlled.

### The Fund That Pays for the Expenditures

Chapter 1 draws the distinction between regular budget and social insurance expenditures and emphasizes that citizens view each type differently. Separating expenditures by the fund that pays for them recognizes these different views (Table 4.2). Increased expenditures on Social Security and the Hospital Insurance component of Medicare make up most of the overall increase in social insurance expenditures. Transfer payments in these programs have grown from 0.6 percent of GDP in 1952 to 6.1 percent in 1993, over 80 percent of the overall percentage increase in total public expenditures. Hence the expenditure categories that have seen the most growth are social insurance funds, which have historically disbursed benefits to workers that have exceeded the workers' payments into the funds.

*Social Security and the Hospital Insurance component of Medicare account for most of the increase in social insurance expenditures.*

Classifying expenditures in this way also brings to light trends in regular budget expenditures that are usually ignored. In particular, public debt at all levels of government lies entirely within regular budgets. Net interest payments have increased by 2.7 percentage points of GDP and exceed all of the increase in regular budgets.

*Interest payments account for the increase in regular budgets.*

Conversely, other programmatic regular budget expenditures have remained essentially constant relative to the economy over the past 41 years, despite great changes in the mix of these expenditures brought on by the decline in defense spending and the rise of other categories shown in Table 4.1.

Table 4.2

CHANGES IN EXPENDITURES BY FUNDING SOURCE

| | Percentage of GDP | | |
|---|---|---|---|
| | 1952 | 1993 | Difference |
| **Total public expenditures** | 26.3 | 33.1 | +6.8 |
| Social insurance | 1.5 | 6.7 | +5.3 |
| Regular budget[a] | 25.3 | 27.7 | +2.4 |
| *Less:* Interfund transactions[b] | −0.4 | −1.3 | −0.9 |

[a]Includes Supplemental Medical Insurance component of Medicare (Medicare B).
[b]Interfund transactions are public employers' contributions to their employees' retirement trust funds. They are regular budget expenditures that become receipts of social insurance funds and, as such, are not public expenditures as defined here. For additional explanation, see Appendix A.

## The Jurisdiction That Undertakes the Expenditure

*An analysis of public expenditures must include state and local expenditures because they are large, . . .*

We have emphasized that any comprehensive analysis of public expenditures must examine both federal and state and local expenditures. At the simplest level, the need to include state and local expenditures in the analysis arises because of the magnitude of these expenditures—in recent years, they have made up more than a third of the total.

*because expenditures are distributed across all levels of governments, . . .*

More important, however, state and local expenditures must be included because of the federal structure of government in the United States. For example, the decline in defense expenditures and the increase in Social Security expenditures have occurred at the federal level of government; growth in expenditures for public education and for police and corrections has occurred at state and local levels; and expenditures on the poor have been shared. Because of this division of effort, looking at federal expenditures in isolation inevitably results in a skewed and partial perspective.

*and because federal grants link expenditures across jurisdictions.*

Finally, it has become critical to include all levels of government in a comprehensive classification of expenditures because federal grants have increasingly linked expenditures across jurisdictions. At the federal level, grants are expenditures, but they are not public expenditures; rather, they are intergovernmental transfers of resources that become receipts of state and local government. The existence of an additional layer of decisionmakers between the grant and the public expenditure means that the functional category of the public expenditure need not correspond in any simple way to that of the grant, if the additional public expenditure occurs at all. This fungibility of federal grants allows state and local governments to substitute across categories of expenditures and thus casts doubt on any accounting of the final ends of federal grants.

Table 4.3 compares federal regular budget expenditures with their state and local counterparts. Net social insurance expenditures, which are entirely federal, are treated in Table 4.2 and hence are omitted here.

Table 4.3

JURISDICTIONAL COMPONENTS OF REGULAR BUDGET EXPENDITURES

| | Percentage of GDP | | |
|---|---|---|---|
| | 1952 | 1993 | Difference |
| **Federal regular budget expenditures** | **19.1** | **17.0** | **−2.0** |
| **Public expenditures** | **18.4** | **14.1** | **−4.3** |
| Defense | 13.2 | 4.8 | −8.4 |
| Net interest payments | 1.6 | 4.2 | +2.6 |
| All other[a] | 3.6 | 5.1 | +1.5 |
| **Grants-in-aid** | **0.7** | **2.9** | **+2.2** |
| **State and local regular budget expenditures** | **7.0** | **13.6** | **+6.6** |
| Net interest payments | 0.1 | 0.1 | +0.1 |
| All other | 6.9 | 13.5 | +6.5 |

[a]Growth in transfer payments for Part B of Medicare makes up 0.9 percentage point of the increase in this category.

In the aggregate, federal regular budget expenditures have fallen relative to the economy, while their state and local analogues have risen to almost half of the regular budget total. Defense expenditures have declined in relative terms by an amount that more than offsets the increase in net interest payments and grants-in-aid, combined with the smaller net increase resulting from a changed mix in all other federal expenditures.

*Federal regular budget expenditures have fallen. State and local regular budget expenditures have grown to almost one-half of the total.*

## Economic Categories of Expenditures

An expenditure's economic type is important for several reasons. First, the type reveals a great deal about the expenditure's effects on other sectors once it is integrated into the economy's income and product flows. Second, the courses of action available to implement policy alternatives differ across economic types of expenditure. For example, direct provision of medical care to veterans through purchases results in far more direct control of expenditures than provision of Medicare transfer payments. Third, an expenditure's type affects a government's ability either to privatize provision of the goods or services giving rise to the expenditure or to subcontract provision to the private sector. This distinction is perhaps especially important at the state and local levels of government. Fourth, the economic type of an expenditure fundamentally affects the degree of potential and actual expenditure control that a government unit can exercise.

*An expenditure's economic type highlights effects in other economic sectors, policy alternatives, and degree of potential expenditure control.*

As we have described above, there are four economic categories of expenditures. These categories and their behavior are shown in Table 4.4. This classification prompts two observations about how these categories have moved over the past 41 years.

74

Table 4.4

CHANGES IN ECONOMIC TYPES OF EXPENDITURES

| | Percentage of GDP | | |
| --- | --- | --- | --- |
| | 1952 | 1993 | Difference |
| **Total public expenditures** | 26.3 | 33.1 | +6.8 |
| Purchases | 21.4 | 18.1 | −3.3 |
| Transfer payments | 4.1 | 14.3 | +10.2 |
| Net interest payments | 1.3 | 1.9 | +0.6 |
| Subsidies less surpluses | −0.1 | 0.1 | +0.2 |
| *Less:* Interfund transactions | −0.4 | −1.3 | −0.9 |

*Growth in government expenditures has occurred as redistributions of income, mainly to the elderly, the poor, and creditors.*

First, public purchases of goods and services made up 18 to 20 percent of GDP over most of the period, despite having peaked twice at nearly 22 percent of GDP during the wars in Korea and Vietnam. (Table 4.4 shows the first peak in 1952.) This category consists of real goods and services that the public sector acquires and uses in its production activities. The table indicates that the magnitude of inputs for these production activities has not grown relative to the economy as a whole. In particular, in those instances where government actually produces and delivers goods to its citizens, expenditures have not grown relative to the economy.

Second, public expenditures other than purchases are components of income, rather than product. All of the relative growth in government expenditures has occurred as redistributions of income through transfer and interest payments, mainly to the elderly, the poor, and creditors.

## IMPLICATIONS FOR POLICY: THE PRESENTATION OF PUBLIC EXPENDITURES

*Alternative budgetary presentations place expenditures in the context of the total economy.*

The four complementary classifications presented in this report offer a coherent view of public expenditures measured relative to the economy. Most notably, they provide a national, multidimensional context for understanding major societal trends and changes that have occurred over the past 41 years. However, these perspectives are seldom presented or used. In particular, they do not surface in presentations of expenditures in the federal budget, nor do they appear in debates about these expenditures.

Since the late 1960s, federal budgetary practice has attempted to focus attention on a one-dimensional, functional view of federal expenditures in the "unified" budget. In recent years, the shortcomings of this approach have been increasingly recognized, and the principle of viewing expenditures in more than one way has again achieved prominence. To date, however, efforts to devise alternative ways of presenting expenditures have focused on federal expenditures alone, thus missing the critical

75

need to place these expenditures within the context of the total public sector and the total economy.

The arguments presented in this report and summarized above suggest that discussion of expenditures in the federal budget should incorporate supplementary presentations that exploit the preceding classification schemes. In particular, these presentations should:

- Separate federal social insurance and regular budget expenditures, focusing on their very different dynamics;

- Emphasize classification of expenditures by their economic type and highlight the different roles of these types in the economy;

- Include a treatment of aggregate state and local expenditures, focusing on their interdependence with federal expenditures through federal grants;

- Recognize that federal grants-in-aid to state and local governments are fungible with other state and local funds; and

- Facilitate decisions on the character of federal expenditures by placing them in the context of total public expenditures.

At a more fundamental level, however, we suggest that the current federal budgetary presentation is flawed at its base. In particular, it does not address the ongoing need for forms of presentation that enhance understanding of public expenditures and facilitate decisions shaping their future. Moreover, alternative budgetary presentations—including those suggested above—are not likely to result in significant progress. Rather, it is time to revisit the basis of how the federal budget is presented and to do so with attention to the fundamentals of budgetary communication and taxonomy.

*It is time for a basic rethinking of how the federal budget is presented.*

## Appendix A

# TREATMENT AND RECONSTRUCTIONS OF DATA FROM THE NATIONAL INCOME AND PRODUCT ACCOUNTS

NIPA data on government expenditures are used throughout this report. This appendix explains instances where our treatments and reconstructions of the NIPA data, and conventions of the data themselves, need clarification. It discusses

- "Government expenditures" in NIPA versus "Public expenditures";
- NIPA's treatment of intergovernmental transactions;
- NIPA's treatment of interfund transactions; and
- Our measurement of public expenditures relative to GDP.

## "GOVERNMENT EXPENDITURES" IN NIPA VERSUS "PUBLIC EXPENDITURES"

The NIPA accounts are designed to represent flows of income and product within the U.S. economy. The most familiar representation of the accounts is in their five numbered summary accounts:

1. National Income and Product;
2. Personal Income and Outlay;
3. Government Receipts and Expenditures;
4. Foreign Transactions; and
5. Gross Saving and Investment.

Although our immediate interest is in the expenditure side of Account 3, all of the NIPA summary accounts are involved in the three reports of this series on U.S. public budgets.

The third account is organized like a budget: It accounts separately for receipts and expenditures, or the sources and uses of funds. However, the government account includes a number of transactions that assist in meeting its primary purpose of representing national product and income, even though these transactions are usually handled differently in budgetary practice. Specifically, NIPA includes some receipts and expenditures that are internal flows within or among governmental units in cases where netting them out would result in loss of data needed to maintain separate product and income flows. In some instances NIPA treats these transactions selectively by including sufficient detail to satisfy the needs of national economic accounting but not enough to allow a full reconciliation of the transactions.

These transactions give rise to an important distinction between government expenditures in NIPA and "public expenditures" in this report. We define public expenditures as government expenditures that flow to other sectors of the economy—i.e., households, businesses, and the rest of the world. The third NIPA account includes both public expenditures and selected inter- and intragovernmental transactions. Thus, NIPA's treatment of the public sector results in a small number of inter- and intragovernmental transactions that require special treatment in this report.

Aside from the transactions discussed in the balance of this appendix, all other expenditure data in this report are drawn directly from NIPA and are hence consistent with the definitions and technical explanations of their derivation contained in BEA (1988). Appendix C contains complete source code for our figures, and any portion of this analysis can be reproduced directly from the NIPA data.

## TREATMENT OF INTERGOVERNMENTAL TRANSACTIONS

Federal grants-in-aid to states and localities are the only intergovernmental transactions identified in NIPA and in this report. These grants are a federal expenditure, but they are not a federal *public* expenditure because they do not flow directly to other sectors of the economy. Rather, they are a transfer of resources to state and local governments, where they are counted as receipts. Hence, federal grants are not included within national aggregate expenditures in NIPA (Table 301); they appear in federal expenditures (Table 302) but not in state and local expenditures, since grants become receipts at these levels of government (Table 303). In Chapter 3 we adhere to the NIPA treatment of federal grants, with the following additional definitional distinction: "federal public expenditures" exclude grants, but "federal expenditures" include them.

An important characteristic of grants that Chapter 3 treats at length is their "fungibility," meaning that the stated purpose of a grant at the federal level need not correspond in any obvious way to how grant funds are ultimately used at the state and local levels. To indicate the approximate effects of grants on the magnitude and trend of state and local expenditures, however, the chapter sometimes shows grants as though they were fully expended as part of state and local public expenditures in the year received.

This convention results in state and local expenditures being partitioned between those financed, in aggregate, by federal grants and those financed by other state and local resources. Moreover, the convention allows us to show the role of grants in expenditure trends of the federal government and of state and local governments. For example, in Figure

3.1b, grants can be viewed as a part of federal expenditures or, alternatively, as a source of finance for total state and local public expenditures for comparison with Figure 3.1a. The convention also appears in Figures 3.4b and 3.12.

## TREATMENT OF INTERFUND TRANSACTIONS

The primary purpose guiding construction of the NIPA government accounts is to provide a sectoral subaccount to the master NIPA account that summarizes the product and income flows of the economy. Consistent with this aim, data in the subordinate accounts are presented to meet the needs of national economic accounting.

The primary purpose of the accounts has a number of implications for how various types of public expenditures are presented. To take an immediate example, the accounts separate social insurance funds from other funds at each jurisdictional level.[1] Despite this separation, however, the NIPA system of accounts does not support a detailed and exhaustive reconciliation among social insurance and other funds, since this reconciliation is not needed for the accounts to fulfill their primary purpose of national income accounting.[2]

Nonetheless, treatments of data that are acceptable for the purposes of NIPA may be substantially at variance with the needs of research on public expenditures. In three situations, reconstructions of NIPA data have been required in order to serve better the specific purposes of this report. These situations involve the NIPA treatments of

- Government employer contributions to government employee retirement;

- The Supplemental Medical Insurance program, or "Part B" of Medicare; and

- Interest earned and paid among various funds in different NIPA tables.

We discuss each of these areas below.

### Government Employer Contributions to Government Employee Retirement

GDP is defined as the market value of the goods and services produced within the United States. Since most goods and services produced in the

---

[1]Details of this separation are contained in NIPA Tables 306, 312, and 314 and in the surpluses and deficits shown in NIPA Tables 301, 302, and 303.

[2]This statement is based on information provided by professional staff members of the Government Division, Bureau of Economic Analysis, Department of Commerce, as described in footnote 3 below.

public sector are not sold in the marketplace, however, market-valued inputs are substituted for market-valued output in calculating GDP. Thus, the government component of GDP is defined as government *purchases* of goods and services.

These purchases include the compensation of government employees, which in turn includes government employer contributions to social insurance funds for government employee retirement. To use the value of inputs for the value of output consistently, government expenditures in NIPA must include these employer contributions in government purchases.

**Contributions netted out of public expenditures.** From the viewpoint of public expenditures, however, these contributions are not part of transactional flows between government and other sectors of the economy; instead, the contributions are diverted into social insurance funds, which are managed by the same government entity that makes the contribution as a trustee. That is, they are intragovernmental, interfund transactions. These transactions are expenditures of the regular budget that pays the employees and receipts of the social insurance budget that makes transfer payments to the employees as benefits upon retirement. The transfer payments from such social insurance retirement funds are public expenditures of the government entity, and they appear in NIPA on the income side of the dual accounting for domestic product and income.

In budgetary practice, intragovernmental, interfund transactions are frequently netted out in calculating total expenditures to avoid double-counting expenditures to the public on a cash-flow basis. However, because these transactions lead to governmental "expenditures" on both the product and income sides of the NIPA accounts, government employer contributions are treated on a gross basis in NIPA (BEA, 1988:18, 81).

The practice of netting these transactions as intragovernmental flows is attractive because it avoids overstatement of expenditures flowing from the government to the public, which is especially important in this report because governments' contributions to their employees' retirement funds have grown relative to the economy over the past 41 years. Thus, gross treatment of these transactions would not only exaggerate the magnitude of actual public expenditures, it would also raise the trend line of their growth.

Netting these transactions is consistent with our definition of public expenditures, and we do so in this report. As a result, all total public expenditures shown in the figures in Chapters 2 and 3 are net of government employer contributions to their employees' retirement funds.

**The several ways of netting.** The functional classification in Chapter 2 includes interfund transactions as part of the purchases included in the individual functions of international and domestic expenditures. The transactions are treated as deductions from the gross amount of transfer payments made to current beneficiaries, thereby resulting in their treatment on a net basis within general government expenditures and within total public expenditures. This convention affects total public expenditures in Figure 2.1 and in Figures 2.7a and 2.7b, which detail the magnitude of government employer contributions by showing their net and gross amounts.

This convention for treating government employer contributions puts the adjustment in one place where it can be explained and presented. Technically, however, it would also be appropriate to deduct the interfund transactions from the magnitude of purchases in each functional category of expenditure and thereby show the individual functional amounts based on the direct flows they generate to other sectors of the economy. Despite being formally correct, this treatment is impractical because it would cause individual functional categories to depart from the values that are readily available in NIPA and would involve a substantial number of technical judgment calls.

The three classifications in Chapter 3 consistently show total public expenditures net of the contributions, while including them in any subordinate detail of the same figure, as necessary. Figures 3.1a and 3.1b are net of contributions both in their totals and by jurisdiction. The total in Figure 3.2 is net of contributions, which are included in purchases and are not netted out of transfers; the contributions are shown separately as a negative expenditure, or a deduction from the total. Likewise, Figure 3.3 shows a net overall total and gross totals for regular and social insurance funds, with government contributions shown as a negative expenditure. Finally, Figure 3.6 applies the approach of Figure 3.3 to federal expenditures, and Figure 3.10 applies the approach of Figure 3.2 to state and local expenditures.

### The Supplemental Medical Insurance Program[3]

When Medicare was enacted in 1965 as a federally sponsored health-insurance program for the aged and disabled, the program was struc-

___
[3]NIPA's treatment of the SMI program was the subject of correspondence and telephone conversations during September and October of 1992 with professional staff members of the Government Division of BEA. These individuals were extraordinarily helpful in clarifying many aspects of this subject and in reviewing and discussing the approach adopted by the authors in this report. Their assistance was especially important because of our interest in maintaining the integrity of the NIPA system of accounts while adopting a different method of treating SMI than that currently followed in NIPA. This treatment includes not only SMI expenditures, but also SMI receipts and surpluses, which will become significant in later reports in this series.

tured in two parts having different and independent means of financing. Part A is Hospital Insurance (HI), financed by the Hospital Insurance Trust Fund; Part B is Supplemental Medical Insurance (SMI), financed by the Supplemental Medical Insurance Trust Fund. Part A was financed by new, compulsory, payroll-based taxes and contributions by employers and employees that resemble finance of the Old Age, Survivors', and Disability Insurance Funds (Social Security). Part B was financed by premiums that were to have been paid by the aged and disabled who voluntarily participated in the insurance plan, as well as by federal government contributions from general revenues.

Within NIPA, the Medicare program and its two trust funds were classified as social insurance funds.[4] A desire to have singular treatment of the Medicare program overrode the distinct differences between the two trust funds.[5] This decision has been followed consistently in NIPA to the present.

**Difficulties in NIPA's treatment of SMI.** NIPA's treatment of SMI has presented three difficulties for the analysis in this report. First, the criteria established for classification of funds as social insurance in NIPA are clearly met by the HI Trust Fund and are just as clearly not met by the SMI Trust Fund. Second, absence of a full reconciliation for interfund transactions within the system of accounts supporting NIPA has resulted in an anomaly: Only SMI premiums from aged and disabled participants are treated as social insurance fund receipts, but all SMI transfer payments are treated as social insurance expenditures. Third, NIPA does not contain enough detail on SMI to allow an alternative treatment based on reconstructed NIPA data. These difficulties are discussed below.

The SMI Trust Fund has a social purpose that is closely allied under Medicare with that of the HI Trust Fund, which is a social insurance fund. Nonetheless, the SMI Trust Fund does not meet the key criterion for social insurance funds in NIPA. BEA (1988:5) states:

> The main resources of [social insurance] funds are derived from compulsory payments—called contributions in the NIPA's—by other sectors and other governmental units.

The SMI Trust Fund has two sources of financing: voluntary premiums paid by current beneficiaries and federal contributions whose amount is determined as part of the disposition of general revenues. Originally, the federal government was to match the voluntary premiums, but in recent years the federal contribution has made up about 70 percent of total

---

[4]*Survey of Current Business*, Department of Commerce, August 1966, p. 6.

[5]This statement is based on recollections by a professional staff member of BEA's Government Division during the conversations and correspondence mentioned in footnote 3 above.

resources. Because participation is optional, SMI lacks the compulsory element that is characteristic of social insurance funds.

In conjunction with the confusion that results from treating the SMI Trust Fund as a social insurance fund, there are accounting difficulties with the current treatment of SMI. The government sector in NIPA lacks a reconciliation of interfund flows between social insurance and other funds. As a consequence, only the voluntary premiums of the beneficiaries are included in receipts of social insurance funds in NIPA Table 314; the federal contribution from general revenues, despite their being the major source of receipts for the SMI Trust Fund, is not recorded as part of social insurance fund receipts in NIPA Table 314. Nonetheless, all SMI transfer payments are included in Table 314. Consequently, the surpluses and deficits shown in NIPA Tables 314, 302, and 301 for social insurance and other funds are erroneous. The surplus in social insurance funds and the deficit in other funds are both understated by the amount of the federal contribution to SMI. Moreover, the error is too large to be ignored: The federal contribution in FY 1993 was $44 billion, or 0.7 percent of GDP.

A final difficulty is that separate data for the two trust funds connected with the Medicare program are not available within NIPA. Thus, NIPA data to support an alternative treatment of SMI cannot be reconstructed solely on the basis of published NIPA data.

**How the data are reconstructed.** The preferred course of action in this report is not to treat SMI as a social insurance fund, as NIPA defines the term. Since participation is voluntary, premiums are paid by current beneficiaries, and the bulk of funding is from federal general revenues, SMI is a trust fund but is not a social insurance fund. To include it as a regular budget trust fund, however, requires a reconstruction of the NIPA data. Absent adequate detail from NIPA sources, we have used federal budgetary sources, specifically OMB (1993). Annual adjustments to the NIPA data are provided as percentages of GDP in Table C.3 of Appendix C.

### Interest Paid and Earned

The treatment of interest payments and earnings differs across the various NIPA tables that cover the government sector. Tables 301, 302, and 303—the three basic government tables—treat interest earnings as negative expenditures, rather than receipts.[6] Table 314, which treats government social insurance funds, regards interest earnings of the funds as receipts. Finally, Tables 315, 316, and 317, which contain a functional classification of government expenditures, treat interest

---

[6]That is, when treated as negative expenditures, interest earnings are offset against any interest payments that exist.

earnings on federal social insurance funds as negative expenditures and interest earnings on state and local social insurance funds as a deduction from the transfer payments of those funds.[7]

To ensure consistency across the figures in this report, data from NIPA Tables 314, 315, and 317 are reconstructed to treat interest earnings as negative expenditures in all cases. Hence, these tables become consistent with the treatment of interest in Tables 301, 302, and 303. Instances in which reconstruction has occurred are shown explicitly in Appendix C.

Finally, dividends that state and local governments receive are merged with interest earnings and are not shown separately in this report. This merger occurs because the magnitude of dividends is too small to warrant separate identification.

## THE RATIO OF PUBLIC EXPENDITURES TO GDP

The NIPA data series map the dual-flow national economy, or the flow of goods and services ("product") and the flow of charges generated in their production ("income"). The two flows are estimated independently, and the estimates are reconciled by allowance for a statistical discrepancy.

A classification of public expenditures by their economic type identifies the side of the dual-flow economy to which a given expenditure belongs. Government purchases are a component of product-side GDP, and transfer payments, net interest payments, and subsidies less surpluses of government enterprises are components of income-side GDP.

In this report, the existence of two-sided accounting for GDP is ignored. We thus follow a convention that is frequently used in discussions of government budgets. Total public expenditures and expenditures within the subcategories of the four expenditure classifications are divided by GDP as if they were part of a one-sided GDP estimate. In fact, government purchases alone represent the public sector's share of GDP, along with consumption, gross private domestic investment, and net exports for the household, business, and rest-of-the-world sectors of the economy, respectively. In forthcoming reports, the distinction between the dual flows, or two sides of the economy, will be emphasized for expenditures, receipts, and surpluses or deficits.

--------

[7]See footnote 2 of Tables 315 and 317.

## Appendix B

# THE EXPENDITURE CLASSIFICATIONS UNDERLYING THIS REPORT

This report classifies total public expenditures by four of their characteristics: the jurisdiction that undertakes the expenditure, the economic type of the expenditure, the fund that pays for it, and its function. A general scheme of classification that is exhaustive with respect to all four characteristics underlies the discussion, but its presentation here is not comprehensive. Rather, we use the underlying classification scheme on a selective basis to meet the immediate purposes of the report.

This appendix explains the nature of the general classification scheme and then describes the steps required to derive the three-way classification by jurisdiction, type, and fund that underlies Chapter 3 and the functional classification that underlies Chapter 2.

## Classification of Public Expenditures

We have developed a general scheme for classifying public expenditures to serve a wide range of purposes in public-policy analysis and budgetary research. In particular, it contributes the upper category levels in a comprehensive expenditures component of a public budgeting taxonomy.

### A Domain for Public Expenditures

The structure of this classification is based on exhaustive cross-classification by the four characteristics of expenditures listed above. It provides a domain for collecting, presenting, and analyzing expenditures for broadly and narrowly based research. Whether one is dealing with macrobudgetary issues (e.g., what functions have contributed most to relative growth?) or microbudgetary issues (e.g., what are the types of expenditures by jurisdiction that support the labor force?), data based on the classification are consistent.

As such, the general classification is designed to discipline the data used in analyses of total public expenditures. At the same time, it is compatible with other components of our public budgetary taxonomy, specifically the components for flows both of public receipts and within credit programs, as well as stocks of assets and liabilities and measures of related quantities. Thus, the definitions, conventions, and reconstructions of data explained in the appendices of this report are consistent with those that will appear for receipts, surpluses, and deficits in subsequent reports in this series.

It is of the utmost importance that the general scheme of classification was developed first, then its portions that would be presented in this report were selected, as described below. This sequence of development is significant because the interpretations and conclusions are based on what the data show, given the methods applied: Prejudged interpretations and conclusions were not the starting point for the design of classifications that would subsequently rationalize them.

The classifications presented in each subsection are mutually exclusive and collectively exhaustive; elements of a classification might be consolidated and not appear, but none are left out or included redundantly. Likewise, the classifications presented are at a level of detail or cross-classification that is of potential interest to the reader, thereby avoiding tedium in the interests of comprehensiveness and limiting the report to a reasonable length.

### Basis and Format of the Classification

We use the NIPA government-sector database in the general classification scheme by reconstructing and extending categories that already exist in the NIPA accounts structure. Hence, we exploit the existing database, rather than creating additional time series, which is unnecessary in this case and can be exceedingly difficult, particularly from the standpoint of validating consistency with existing data. Importantly, this permits use of the expenditures component and other components of the classification in conjunction with private-sector NIPA data. Thus, public expenditures can be examined within and among the public and private sectors of the total economy.

Although the general classification of public expenditures is based on four characteristics, it can be represented in a two-dimensional format by presenting the functional classification in the rows and cross-classification by jurisdiction, fund, and type in the requisite number of columns. The existing structure of the relevant NIPA tabulations is sufficient to saturate this format.

### The Part of the Classification Used in This Report

This generalized format, for each of the 42 calendar years since 1952, underlies the data presented in this report. However, only a very limited amount of the available data is used: Specifically, there is no cross-classification by all four characteristics—Chapter 2 considers only the function of expenditures; treatment of the other three characteristics appears in Chapter 3. In addition, the graphical presentations in each chapter are not exhaustive. Chapter 2 presents many of the functions at a level well above the elements of which they are composed, and in Chapter 3 only a portion of the possible cross-classifications is shown.

## Classification of Expenditures by Jurisdiction, Economic Type, and Fund

Strictly speaking, the government accounts of NIPA do not present government budgets. Rather, data from budgetary sources are translated for inclusion in NIPA's representation of product and income flows. The accounts cover only past years, in contrast to public budgets, which typically present a single past year and include a plan that covers the current year and one or more future years to facilitate government fiscal planning and other activities. Nonetheless, we use the term "NIPA budgets" as shorthand for conveying the source and character of the data.

## NIPA's Nine Expenditure Budgets

Chapter 3 uses these data to examine public expenditures along three dimensions. Cross-classification by jurisdiction (national, federal, and state and local) and fund (aggregate, regular, and social insurance) yields nine expenditure budgets, each of which contains subordinate classifications by economic type of transaction.

National, federal, and state and local jurisdictions are presented by type of transaction in NIPA Tables 301, 302, and 303, respectively. Federal and state and local social insurance budgets are presented by type of transaction in NIPA Table 314; the entries can be summed to obtain the national social insurance budget. Although data for other "regular budget" funds are not provided in publicly available NIPA sources, they can be calculated by subtracting social insurance from aggregate budgets. The resulting nine expenditure budgets, with their source tables in NIPA, are displayed schematically in Figure B.1. The figures of Chapter 3 cover, in varying levels of detail, all nine expenditure budgets shown in this figure. The mapping between budgets and figures is shown in Figure B.2.

## The Effects of Intergovernmental and Interfund Transactions

Although these budgets are derived essentially from the four NIPA tables mentioned above, their analysis has required several adjustments to NIPA's treatment of intergovernmental and interfund transactions. Appendix A discusses these in detail, but it is worth explaining here the effects of these transactions on the nine expenditure budgets. All of these reconstructions are explicitly identified in the source code of Appendix C.

|  | Aggregate | Regular | Social insurance |
|---|---|---|---|
| National | T301 | Derived | Derived |
| Federal | T302 | Derived | T314 |
| State and local | T303 | Derived | T314 |

**Figure B.1—Major Source Tables Within NIPA**

|  | Aggregate | Regular | Social insurance |
|---|---|---|---|
| National | 3.1a, 3.1b<br>3.2<br>3.3 | 3.4a, 3.4b | 3.5 |
| Federal | 3.6 | 3.7a, 3.7b<br>3.8 | 3.9a, 3.9b |
| State and local | 3.10 | 3.11a, 3.11b<br>3.12 | 3.13 |

**Figure B.2—Classification of Figures in Chapter 3**

**Intergovernmental transactions.** Intergovernmental transactions—namely, federal grants—affect the columns in Figures B.1 and B.2 that correspond to aggregate and regular budgets. If grants are deducted from Table 302, the resulting total corresponds to federal public expenditures, which are added to state and local expenditures (Table 303) to form total, or "national," public expenditures, shown in Table 301.[1] Grants appear in Figures 3.1b, 3.4b, 3.7b, and 3.12.

---

[1]Appendix A discusses the concept of "public expenditures" in detail.

**Interfund transactions.** Interfund transactions affect all rows in Figures B.1 and B.2. There are three types of interfund transaction that require discussion in this appendix: government employer contributions to their employees' retirement funds, our treatment of expenditures from the SMI trust fund, and net interest payments.

Government employer contributions to government employee social insurance funds are deducted from each entry in the "Aggregate" column because these contributions do not flow directly to other sectors of the economy; rather, they are included in each row of the "Regular" column as purchase expenditures. Consequently, the sum of the expenditures shown for regular and social insurance budgets in each row exceeds the entry for the aggregate budget in that row.

The rationale for our treatment of expenditures from the SMI trust fund is given in Appendix A. In brief, we have reconstructed the NIPA data to make these expenditures part of the federal regular budget. As a result, in the "Federal" and "National" rows these expenditures supplement regular budget totals and are removed from social insurance totals, while the aggregate remains constant.

Net interest payments are treated by reconstructing Table 314 to show interest and dividends on social insurance funds consistently as negative expenditures, which is how they appear in Tables 301, 302, and 303. We use the resulting Table 314 to derive social insurance and regular budget expenditures for each row in Figures B.1 and B.2.

Our treatment of interfund transactions affects each figure in Chapter 3. Additionally, the treatment of government employer contributions to government employee social insurance funds affects Figures 2.1, 2.4a, and 2.4b.

## Classification of Expenditures by Function

NIPA Tables 315, 316, and 317 present a functional classification of government expenditures. The national-level classification in Table 315 uses 21 categories with no subcategories or functional elements and no classification by the economic type of transaction. The classification of federal expenditures in Table 316 uses 20 of the 21 national categories, with four subcategories and 58 functional elements. The table's columns cross-classify expenditures by four transaction types but combine net interest and transfer payments. Table 317 uses 17 of the 21 national categories to classify state and local expenditures; it contains no subcategories, but it has 29 functional elements. Like its analogue for federal expenditures, this table's columns cross-classify expenditures by economic type, with net interest and transfer payments combined.

Our classification relies on the NIPA functional elements and hence is in no sense a fresh start at the problems posed by functional expenditure classification. We view it more as a useful rearrangement of the available data. As the balance of this appendix indicates, our classification scheme requires substantial reconstruction of NIPA's scheme and subsequent validation of its control totals. The discussion of this reconstruction and validation proceeds in four steps:

- Critique of NIPA's functional classification;

- Augmentation of the NIPA functional elements;

- Discussion of the major steps in data reconstruction; and

- Description of the reconstructed functional classification.

### A Critique of NIPA's Functional Classification

The existing NIPA national classification of expenditures by function has several defects that led us to rearrange the detailed information contained in Tables 316 and 317.

NIPA's functional classification of expenditures for 1952 and 1993 is shown in Table B.1. Several features of this classification stand out. First, there are evident disparities across the magnitudes of expenditures in the various categories. Specifically, since six categories do not exceed 0.25 percent of GDP in either 1952 or 1993, a more aggregated scheme might aid understanding of underlying trends.

Likewise, two categories—"National defense" and "Income support, Social Security, and welfare (ISSSW)"—are very large relative to other categories in both years. The size of the national-defense category is understandable, since the category represents a large, fairly homogeneous group of expenditures. However, the ISSSW category is really a misnomer, since it includes Social Security; Medicare; state and local medical care, including Medicaid grants; Unemployment Insurance; government employee retirement; and a variety of programs that aid the poor. As the analysis in Chapter 2 suggests, these categories of expenditure have had very different dynamics and underlying determinants since 1952, and their aggregation thus obscures more than it clarifies.

Second, the ostensibly national categories in the table have a distinctly federal flavor. In general terms, this is suggested by four of the categories describing expenditures undertaken only by the federal government (international affairs, space, national defense, and the Postal Service), and only one dealing with uniquely state and local expenditures (commercial activities).[2] Moreover, only state and local expenditures appear in the "unallocable" category.

---

[2]This bias reflects the underlying differences in detail in Tables 316 and 317. The federal-expenditure classification in the first table has nearly twice as many lines as the state and local classification in the second.

Table B.1

NIPA FUNCTIONAL CLASSIFICATION OF EXPENDITURES AS
PERCENTAGES OF GDP, 1952 AND 1993

|  | 1952 | 1993 |
|---|---|---|
| Central executive, legislative, and judicial | 0.86 | 1.20 |
| International affairs | 0.65 | 0.32 |
| Space | 0.00 | 0.22 |
| National defense | 13.18 | 4.77 |
| Civilian safety | 0.60 | 1.45 |
| Education | 2.35 | 5.27 |
| Health and hospitals | 0.62 | 0.65 |
| Income support, Social Security, and welfare | 2.33 | 14.13 |
| Veterans' benefits and services | 1.63 | 0.62 |
| Housing and community services | 0.37 | 0.54 |
| Recreational and cultural activities | 0.09 | 0.23 |
| Energy | 0.08 | 0.06 |
| Agriculture | 0.35 | 0.42 |
| Natural resources | 0.32 | 0.26 |
| Transportation | 1.54 | 1.47 |
| Postal Service | 0.24 | 0.04 |
| Economic development, regulation, and services | 0.09 | 0.16 |
| Labor training and services | 0.07 | 0.13 |
| Commercial activities | −0.05 | −0.15 |
| Net interest paid | 1.28 | 1.89 |
| Other and unallocable | 0.18 | 0.76 |
| Total NIPA government expenditures | 26.74 | 34.45 |
| Less government employer contributions to government employee retirement[a] | 0.40 | 1.32 |
| Total public expenditures | 26.34 | 33.13 |

[a]Deduction of these contributions to arrive at total public expenditures is consistent with the definition used throughout the report.

Perhaps the best evidence that the classification leans toward a federal perspective, however, is the existence of a separate category for veterans' benefits and services. Because this category includes income support, education, and health benefits, it causes expenditures in these three other functional categories to be understated. In addition, a separate category for veterans' benefits implies the lack of consistent criteria for establishing a category and for maintaining categories as mutually exclusive.

*Augmenting NIPA's Set of Functional Elements*

Elements used to construct our functional classification were drawn primarily from Tables 316 and 317. However, NIPA Table 312 provides a more detailed set of elements for transfer payments to individuals than either of these tables, elements that include several programs of general interest not shown separately in the major source tables. Hence, a full reconciliation between Tables 312, 316, and 317 lets us augment the detail on transfer payments in Chapter 2.

This reconciliation involves two technical difficulties. First, coverage differs across Tables 312 and 316. The first table covers transfer payments only to individuals in the United States, whereas the second covers all federal transfer payments, including those to the rest of the world.[3] Second, the entries of Table 312 are in billions of dollars and those of Tables 316 and 317 are in millions of dollars, so their reconciliation results in minor roundoff errors.

In Table 316, the reconciliation allows a more detailed program identification to substitute for lines 44 ("Welfare and social services") and 45 ("Other income support, Social Security, and welfare"). Similarly, in Table 317 it allows enhanced detail for line 21 ("Welfare and social services"). As a result, the augmented database provides separate identification of four significant programs:

- Supplemental Security Income;
- Earned Income Credit;
- Food Stamp program; and
- Aid to Families with Dependent Children.

These programs appear in Figures 2.16, 2.18, and 2.20.

### The Major Steps in Data Reconstruction

Our reclassification of functional expenditures is designed to allow exhaustive cross-classification with other classifications discussed in this appendix. To ensure this possibility, four reconstructions of the data are necessary.

- *In Table 317 we separate transfer payments from interest earnings.*

Table 317 deducts interest earnings from transfer payments in state and local social insurance funds; it shows only the net result in the relevant lines of its combined transfer and interest-payment column, as explained in the table's footnote 2. This treatment is inconsistent with the separation of interest earnings and transfer payments in Table 316 (federal social insurance funds), Table 314 (state and local social insurance funds), and Table 303 (state and local expenditures and receipts). We have therefore eliminated the anomaly in Table 317 and separated transfer payments from interest earnings, treated as negative expenditures; in this way, we ensured that each could be used separately in the functional classification.

---

[3]Transfers to the rest of the world include some transfers to individuals, such as Social Security benefits paid to persons living outside the United States, and all transfers to foreign governments.

- *Using this result, we display separate columns for transfer and interest payments in each of the four tables.*

- *Table 312 is reconciled with Tables 316 and 317 to provide augmented functional elements for transfer payments, as discussed above.*

- *The functional elements in the regular and social insurance budgets are separated.[4]*

**Residual problems.** After these steps were completed, several difficulties remained before the revised Tables 316 and 317 could be summed and rearranged to arrive at our new national functional classification. First, our national classification is composed of individual functional elements from the federal and state and local tables; hence, at the national level, elements had to be imposed in instances where the federal and state and local elements are not identical. For example, the state and local table displays detail for "Health" and "Hospitals" separately, but the federal table shows only the composite category "Health and hospitals." Consequently, it was necessary to combine the detailed state and local elements in the national summation. Similarly, the federal table shares some elements of the "Education" category with its state and local analogue. However, elements unique to each jurisdiction were necessarily combined into an imposed "Other education" national-level element.

Second, there are elements throughout the federal and state and local tables that may have merited attention in the past but have little or no significance today. A prime example is the separate identification of federal "Civil defense" expenditures as an element of "National defense."[5] Regardless of the irrelevance of such elements to the broad consideration of public expenditures, we have retained them in our classification scheme to ensure that the scheme remains collectively exhaustive in subsequent manipulations.

Finally, expenditures are combined in some instances where separate identification would be useful. In some cases, we were able to expand elements by reconciliation to more detailed NIPA sources, as discussed in the case of transfer payments above. However, there are other cases of considerable interest where no additional detail can be found within NIPA. An example is expenditures for the judiciary, which NIPA combines with legislative and central executive expenditures. As a result, judicial expenditures cannot be identified separately for comparison with expenditures on police and corrections. In the critical instance of the SMI program, we have augmented NIPA from budgetary sources, as explained in Appendix A. With this one exception, however,

[4]The last step is significant, since it makes the detailed functional classification useful in broader research on public budgets.

[5]In 1991, civil defense expenditures amounted to $262 million, yet they are a separate subcategory of the $326-billion NIPA national-defense category.

the level of detail in our classification is limited by that available in NIPA.

*A Description of the Reconstructed Functional Classification*

One way of looking at budgeting is as a two-way flow of information—from the totals to the details and from the details to the totals (Mosher, 1954:3). This conception is fundamental in budgetary design, and we have used it in devising our functional classification. At the highest level of aggregation—in the major categories of the classification—we have sought to distinguish among the broadest functions of public expenditures. At the lowest level of aggregation—in its detailed elements—we have sought to cluster elements of expenditure that could be viewed as substitutes or complements. Our interest in this approach goes beyond the immediate need to classify public expenditures and addresses our desire for a classification scheme that is useful more broadly in public policy analysis and public budgetary research. In addition, working in both directions between details and totals makes several useful intermediate levels of aggregation apparent.

Table B.2 shows the major categories, groupings, and categories of expenditures as percentages of GDP that result from this process for 1952 and 1993. After a brief comparison with the existing NIPA functional classification, we describe the components of our classification to the element level.

**The new functional classification relative to NIPA.** NIPA's functional classification has three levels, which we label in descending order "categories," "subcategories," and "elements"; it makes minimal use of the second level, however. When fully extended, our functional classification has six levels that contain more higher-level aggregations and lower-level intermediate aggregations. Table B.2 presents our three highest levels, with "major categories" in boldface type, "groupings" in italics, and "categories" in roman type. Our categories are comparable to the NIPA categories shown in Table B.1.

Although the two classification schemes have a number of categories in common, the number of categories falls from 21 in NIPA to 14 in our scheme, since we combine several of the minor NIPA categories by reducing them to subcategory status or lower. As a result, the smallest categories make up at least 0.40 percent of GDP in either 1952 or 1993.

At the same time, the reduction in categories results in a table no larger than the NIPA display, but one containing higher-level aggregations—specifically, the four major categories and the groupings under the "Domestic" major category. These additional levels of aggregation provide insights not apparent within the NIPA classification. Moreover, they shift perception of the largest expenditure components away from NIPA's "National defense" and "ISSSW" categories and toward our

Table B.2

REVISED FUNCTIONAL CLASSIFICATION OF EXPENDITURES AS
PERCENTAGES OF GDP, 1952 AND 1993

|  | 1952 | 1993 |
|---|---|---|
| **International** | **13.83** | **5.12** |
| National defense | 13.18 | 4.80 |
| Other international | 0.65 | 0.32 |
| | | |
| **Domestic** | **10.44** | **24.31** |
| | | |
| *Basic programs:* | *5.63* | *13.65* |
| Education | 2.58 | 5.28 |
| Health | 0.91 | 5.42 |
| Transportation | 1.54 | 1.48 |
| Civilian safety | 0.60 | 1.45 |
| | | |
| *Support programs:* | *4.17* | *9.84* |
| Support of individuals | 2.73 | 7.03 |
| Support of the economy | 1.00 | 1.75 |
| Support of the labor force | 0.44 | 1.06 |
| | | |
| *Other programs:* | *0.65* | *0.82* |
| Utilities and commercial activities | 0.47 | 0.06 |
| Unallocable | 0.18 | 0.76 |
| | | |
| **Financial** | **1.28** | **1.89** |
| Net interest paid | 1.28 | 1.89 |
| | | |
| **General** | **0.80** | **1.82** |
| Central activities | 0.86 | 1.20 |
| Net retirement | −0.05 | 0.62 |
| | | |
| **Total** | **26.34** | **33.13** |

"International" and "Domestic" categories, which is where the fundamental distinctions lie.

**Details on the revised functional classification.**   We now turn to description of our functional classification, limiting ourselves to those aspects of the scheme most relevant to the text.   This description emphasizes, first, the identification of NIPA elements and, second, identification of elements at various levels of aggregation that provide a point of departure for near-term policy analyses.

The major categories of the classification scheme were designed to separate *program* expenditures from both *financial* and *general* expenditures and to divide program expenditures between international and domestic functions.   Three of the four major categories—"International," "Financial," and "General expenditures"—have relatively simple subordinate structures.

The major category of "Domestic" expenditures is more complex, however, since it contains both the bulk of the functions and 70 percent of the total expenditures in 1993. As a result, this major category has major groupings as well as categories within its upper levels of aggregation. Chapter 2 describes in general terms this breakdown of domestic expenditures into "Basic programs," "Support of individuals," "Support of the economy," "Support of the labor force," and "Other expenditures." Construction of these aggregate categories from less-aggregated elements was guided by a series of questions:

- Would aggregation of the functional elements in question collect substitutes or complements?

- Are there historical reasons for aggregating or separating the elements?

- Do these historical factors remain relevant today?

- If not, are there current reasons for their existence as separate functions of public expenditures?

- Would the relocation of a functional element aid the conduct of policy analysis?

Table B.3 shows the elements and intermediate aggregation levels of the resulting functional classification and identifies the NIPA table and line references from which they are derived. The term "calc." is used to identify imposed elements, as well as aggregations that are the sum of subordinate elements and are thus subject to adjustments resulting from effects of the various reconstructions discussed above.[6]

*International programs.* The major category "International programs" retains the two categories of the NIPA functional classification. Its only change is addition of "Military medical insurance," which surfaced in the reconciliation of Tables 316 and 317 with Table 312. This major category consists exclusively of federal expenditures. Analytically, it juxtaposes conduct of diplomatic and military operations, as well as economic and military foreign assistance.

*Domestic programs.* The major category "Domestic programs" uses the three groupings discussed above: "Basic programs," "Support programs," and "Other programs."

*Basic programs.* This grouping contains four categories:

- "Education" merges elements of the NIPA "Education" category. The only change is addition of the "Veterans' education" element, which is included in the NIPA category "Veterans' benefits and services."

---

[6]All of these adjustments are minor, and most of them involve disposition of rounding errors.

Table B.3

FULL DISPLAY OF FUNCTIONAL CLASSIFICATION WITH TABLE AND LINE
REFERENCES FOR FUNCTIONAL ELEMENTS

INTERNATIONAL PROGRAMS
| | |
|---|---|
| calc. | National defense |
| 316.12 | Military activities |
| 316.13 | Civil defense |
| 316.14 | Foreign military assistance |
| 312.18 | Military medical insurance |
| 316.15 | Other national defense |
| 316.7 | International affairs |
| 316.8 | Conduct of foreign affairs & international activities |
| 316.9 | Foreign economic assistance |

DOMESTIC PROGRAMS
| | |
|---|---|
| calc. | *Basic programs* |
| calc. | Education |
| calc. | Elementary and secondary education |
| 316.21 | Elementary and secondary education |
| 317.10 | Elementary and secondary education |
| calc. | Higher education |
| 316.22 | Higher education |
| 317.11 | Higher education |
| 316.48 | Veterans' education |
| calc. | Other education |
| 316.23 | General research and other education |
| 317.12 | Libraries |
| 317.13 | Other education |
| calc. | Health |
| 316.42 | Hospital and supplementary medical ins. (Medicare) |
| created | Hospital insurance (Medicare) |
| created | Supplemental medical insurance (Medicare) |
| calc. | State and local medical care |
| 317.20 | Medical care |
| 316.43 | Medicaid |
| calc. | Health and hospitals |
| 316.24 | Health and hospitals |
| 317.14 | Health and hospitals |
| 317.15 | Health |
| 317.16 | Hospitals |
| 316.50 | Veterans' hospitals and medical care |
| calc. | Transportation |
| calc. | Highways |
| 316.68 | Highways |
| 317.35 | Highways |
| calc. | Water transportation |
| 316.69 | Water transportation |
| 317.36 | Water transportation |
| calc. | Air transportation |
| 316.70 | Air transportation |
| 317.37 | Air transportation |
| calc. | Transit and railroad transportation |
| 316.71 | Railroad transportation |
| 316.72 | Transit transportation |
| 317.38 | Transit and railroad |

| | |
|---|---|
| calc. | Civilian safety |
| calc. | Police |
| 316.17 | Police |
| 317.6 | Police |
| calc. | Fire |
| 316.18 | Fire |
| 317.7 | Fire |
| calc. | Corrections |
| 316.19 | Corrections |
| 317.8 | Corrections |
| | |
| calc. | *Support programs* |
| | |
| calc. | Support of individuals |
| calc. | Social security (OASDI) |
| 316.27 | Old-age and survivors insurance |
| 316.32 | Disability insurance |
| calc. | Supplementary security income |
| 312.25 | Supplementary security income |
| 312.36 | Supplemental security income |
| calc. | Railroad retirement and disability |
| 316.30 | Railroad retirement |
| 316.35 | Railroad disability |
| calc. | Veterans' income support and services |
| 316.47 | Veterans' disability and survivors compensation |
| 316.49 | Veterans' insurance |
| 316.51 | Veterans' other benefits and services |
| 317.22 | Veterans' benefits and services |
| calc. | Welfare and social services |
| 312.35 | Aid to families with dependent children |
| 312.23 | Food stamp benefits |
| calc. | Other welfare and social services |
| 312.24 | Black lung benefits |
| 312.26 | Direct relief |
| 312.37 | General assistance |
| 316.44 | Welfare and social services* |
| 316.45 | Other income support, Social Security, and welfare* |
| 317.21 | Welfare and social services* |
| | |
| calc. | Support of the economy |
| calc. | Agriculture, natural resources and energy |
| calc. | Agriculture |
| 316.62 | Stabilization of farm prices and income |
| 316.63 | Financing farm ownership and utilities |
| 316.64 | Conservation of agricultural resources |
| 316.65 | Other agriculture |
| 317.32 | Agriculture |
| | |
| calc. | Natural resources |
| 316.66 | Natural resources |
| 317.33 | Natural resources |
| | |
| calc. | Energy |
| 312.38 | Energy assistance |
| 316.58 | Conservation and development of energy sources |
| 316.60 | Administration and regulation |
| | |
| calc. | Economic development, housing, recreational and cultural activities |

| | |
|---|---|
| calc. | Economic development, regulation, and services |
| 3.16.75 | Economic development assistance |
| 3.16.76 | Regulation of commerce and finance |
| 3.16.77 | Other economic development, regulation, and services |
| 3.17.39 | Economic development, regulation, and services |
| calc. | Housing, community development, and urban renewal |
| 3.16.53 | Urban renewal and community development |
| 3.16.54 | Housing |
| 3.17.24 | Housing, community development, and urban renewal |
| | |
| calc. | Recreational and cultural activities |
| 316.56 | Recreational and cultural activities |
| 317.28 | Recreational and cultural activities |
| | |
| 316.10 | Space |
| | |
| calc. | Support of the labor force |
| 3.16.37 | Unemployment insurance |
| 3.16.38 | Regular unemployment insurance |
| 3.16.39 | Extended unemployment insurance |
| 3.16.40 | Other unemployment insurance |
| calc. | Workers' compensation and temp. disability ins. |
| 312.17 | Workers' compensation |
| 312.32 | Temporary disability insurance |
| 312.33 | Workers' compensation |
| calc. | Labor training and services |
| 316.79 | Training programs |
| 316.80 | Other labor services |
| 317.40 | Labor training and services |
| 312.27 | Earned income credit |
| 312.15 | Pension benefit guaranty |
| | |
| calc. | *Other programs* |
| | |
| calc. | Utilities and commercial activities |
| calc. | Utilities |
| 316.59 | Production and sale of power |
| 317.30 | Gas utilities |
| 317.31 | Electric utilities |
| 316.55 | Water and sewerage |
| 317.25 | Water service |
| 317.26 | Sewerage |
| 317.27 | Sanitation |
| calc. | Commercial activities |
| 316.73 | Postal service |
| 317.42 | Publicly owned liquor store systems |
| 317.43 | Government administered lotteries and pari-mutuels |
| 317.44 | Other commercial activities |
| calc. | Other and unallocable |
| 316.82 | Revenue sharing |
| 317.46 | Other and unallocable |
| calc. | Round-offs and residuals |
| | |
| FINANCIAL | |
| calc. | Net interest paid |
| 316.81 | Net interest paid (federal) |
| calc. | Net interest paid (federal regular budget) |
| 314.7 | Less: Interest received (federal SI funds) |
| calc. | Net interest paid (state and local) |
| 317.45 | Net interest paid (state and local regular budget) |

| | |
|---|---|
| 314.18 | Less: Interest and dividends received (state and local SI funds) |
| | |
| GENERAL | |
| calc. | Central activities |
| calc. | Administrative, legislative, and judicial activities |
| 316.5 | Legislative and judicial activities |
| 316.3 | Central administration and management |
| 317.3 | Administrative, legislative, and judicial activities |
| calc. | Tax collection and financial management |
| 316.4 | Tax collection and financial management |
| 317.4 | Tax collection and financial management |
| 316.6 | Other |
| | |
| calc. | Net retirement of government employees |
| calc. | Gross retirement and disability |
| calc. | Military employees retirement and disability |
| 316.29 | Federal government employees retirement, military |
| 316.34 | Federal government employees disability, military |
| calc. | Federal civilian employees retirement and disability |
| 316.28 | Federal government employees retirement, civilian |
| 316.33 | Federal government employees disability, civilian |
| 317.18 | State and local employees retirement and disability |
| calc. | Less: Government employer contributions to government employee retirement |
| 306.14 | Military employees |
| 306.13 | Federal civilian employees |
| 306.19 | State and local employee retirement |

*Residuals after reconciliation with Table 312.

- "Health" has been expanded substantially and includes the NIPA category for "Health and hospitals," plus three other major programs located elsewhere in the NIPA classification—"Veterans' hospitals and medical care" from the "Veterans' benefits and services category"; Medicare from ISSSW; and "State and local medical care," including Medicaid programs, from ISSSW. Expansion of the "Health" category facilitates analyses of this major area of policy concern.

- "Transportation" merges elements of the corresponding NIPA categories without change.

- Likewise, "Civilian safety" merges elements of the corresponding NIPA categories without change.

*Support programs.* Within the support programs grouping of domestic programs, there are three new categories that rearray most of the remaining functional categories and elements of the NIPA classification.

- "Support of individuals" includes programs that provide benefits and services to specific individuals that are unrelated to their current employment, excluding retirement and disability benefits for public employees, which are in the major category of general expenditures.

The first four subcategories of "Support of individuals" relate mainly to retirement and disability. The fifth, "Supplemental Security Income," emerged when we reconciled Table 312 with Tables 316 and 317; it is clustered with the four preceding subcategories to facilitate analyses of Social Security. The final subcategory ("Welfare and social services") includes major programs from the reconciliation with Table 312, as well as residuals of the three elements contained in NIPA's ISSSW category. Addition of elements from Table 312 permits this subcategory to present two major welfare programs—AFDC and the Food Stamp program— that are not shown separately in Tables 316 and 317.

- "Support of the economy" includes a wide variety of relatively small programs that are concerned with economic resources.

These subcategories are often treated as separate national functions. However, because they tend to be very small, especially when measured relative to the economy, and have common characteristics, we present them in a way that allows them to be tracked at several levels of aggregation.

The subcategory "Agriculture, natural resources, and energy" collects programs that are concerned with various types of nonmanufactured resources and that have their greatest effects in rural areas. The subcategory "Economic development, housing, and recreational and cultural activities" collects, for the most part, programs oriented toward manufactured resources and public goods and services affecting mainly urban areas. "Space" is included as a subcategory because the program is too small to merit separate treatment, but it has evolved toward significance in various fields of economic activity, such as communications and meteorology.

In general, imposed elements and source elements below the subcategory level in our classification scheme correspond to those in the major NIPA categories. The only clear exception to this statement concerns the "Energy" subcategory. The federal element for "Production and sale of power" and the state and local elements for "Gas utilities" and "Electric utilities" have been shifted to the category of "Other programs," as explained below. The "Energy assistance" program, which surfaced in the reconciliation of Tables 316 and 317 to Table 312, has been placed in the "Energy" subcategory to facilitate its analysis with the "Conservation and development of energy sources" program, another element of the category.

- "Support of the labor force" includes NIPA's "Labor training and services" category, along with four other labor-force-related programs housed in ISSSW in the NIPA classification.

This category includes two programs that provide support during periods of temporary unemployment and work-related disablement— Unemployment Insurance and Workers' Compensation and Temporary Disability Insurance.

It also includes two programs that encourage employment—"Labor training and services" and the Earned Income Credit. The Pension Benefit Guaranty Program is a small item that surfaced, along with the Earned Income Credit, in the reconciliation to Table 312.

*Other programs.* Finally, the "Other programs" grouping includes without change the "Commercial activities" and the "Other" and "Unallocable" categories from the NIPA classification, except for inclusion of the Postal Service among commercial activities.

It also contains a new subcategory, "Utilities," which collects seven elements appearing in various NIPA categories that are part of "Support of the economy" within our classification. There are at least two reasons for locating these elements within other programs: First, the elements represent programs that are typically government enterprises and appear in NIPA mainly in terms of current operating surpluses or deficits. When these programs are included in support of the economy, their surpluses offset expenditures and thereby disguise program size. For example, the three elements "Production and sale of power," "Gas utilities," and "Electric utilities" are included in the "Energy" category in NIPA and cause that category to become negative in many years (Table B.1). By collecting these elements in "Utilities," we isolate these government enterprises from other categories that they would otherwise distort.

Second, the "Utilities and commercial activities" category brings together the elements of public expenditure that compete most directly with private business in providing services and are hence the most plausible candidates for privatization.

*Financial expenditures.* The major category "Financial expenditures" is the NIPA category for net interest paid. Treatment of these expenditures separately serves several purposes. First, it separates expenditures primarily related to past accumulation of both debt in regular budgets and assets in social insurance budgets from expenditures associated with the present conduct of international and domestic programs. Second, the separation facilitates examination of budgets by jurisdiction and fund by excluding interest earned and paid, both of which involve substantial interfund transactions. Finally, NIPA records only flows of product and income in the economy—in this instance, interest flows. The major category of "Financial expenditures" is the point where our classification can be extended to include other financial aspects of public budgeting that are not part of the NIPA flows—specifically, changes in stocks of assets and liabilities as a result of various other financial activities of government. These include loans, loan guarantees, and deposit-insurance payments (e.g., payment of deposit insurance on failed thrift institutions). Thus, it is a bridge that leads beyond NIPA for certain types of budgetary research.

*General expenditures.* The major category "General expenditures" contains two "overhead" categories. First, "Central activities" retains without change the NIPA category for "Administrative, legislative and judicial activities."

Second, the category contains retirement and disability social insurance programs for public employees on a net basis. The latter programs are collected here, since they entail a number of difficulties from a public accounting standpoint. In the first instance, the expenditures are an overhead labor expense for government, similar to other forms of nonwage compensation paid by private businesses. Even though the government includes its contributions among its purchases, and they are hence already counted in the totals for "International and domestic programs," the contributions are interfund transactions, not public expenditures. As Appendix A explains in detail, we deduct these contributions from NIPA total expenditures throughout this report.

In the second instance, these programs can affect trends in public expenditures idiosyncratically because government, unlike most private businesses, acts as its own trustee and manager for these funds. As trustee, it pays benefits as "public" expenditures, which are financed partially by the contributions of employees and interest and dividend earnings on reserves. Consequently, public expenditures may be rising due to greater retirement payments even in times when the government contributions to partially finance these programs are steady or falling in relative terms.

For both of these reasons, we locate these public employee retirement programs in the "General" major category so that they may be treated in the manner appropriate to a given line of inquiry.

## Appendix C

## SOURCE CODE FOR FIGURES DERIVED FROM NIPA

This appendix documents the reproducibility of each figure derived from NIPA in this report. For an explanation of how these figures were generated, see Chapter 1 and Appendices A and B.

The source information for each figure is formatted as follows: The legends, as they appear on the figure, are provided in the first column, and NIPA references appear in the second. All NIPA references are shown as "TxxxLxxx"with T standing for Table and L for Line. Entries involving more than one line are shown as simple multiterm formulas. Although GDP (T101L1) is used as a divisor throughout the figures, it is not shown in each entry.

### SOURCE CODE FOR CHAPTER 2

The source code for figures in Chapter 2 appears in Table C.1. In instances where NIPA has a line that summarizes other lines, it is used, when applicable, instead of the more detailed listing given in our classification (Table B.3 of Appendix B). For example, the summary line for "National Defense" (T316L11) is used in Table C.1 in place of lines T316L12 through T316L15, shown in Table B.3. This procedure shortens the source code, while still documenting our functional classification.

Appendix B explains the reconstructions of NIPA data involved in constructing our functional classification, including the eventual disposition of roundings and other minor adjustments. The minor adjustments—but clearly not the reconstructions—are ignored in Table C.1. Their magnitudes are very small, individually less than 0.1 percent of GDP, and they therefore have little effect on the figures.

Where applicable, federal grants are excluded from the figures in Chapter 2. Our reconciliation between funds forms the basis for Figure 2.3 because amounts for gross interest paid and received in Tables 302 and 303 are not available between 1952 and 1958. Some of the codes for summary figures refer to the total lines of subordinate figures. This procedure indicates linkages among the figures, while shortening the source code.

### SOURCE CODE FOR CHAPTER 3

Finally, the source code for figures in Chapter 3 appears in Table C.2. In those instances where the SMI fund is shifted from the federal social insurance to the federal regular budget, the format "SMI(xxx)" appears. It refers to the individual columns of Table C.3. Procedures similar to those employed in Table C.1 and described above are used where they shorten the source code.

Table C.1

IDENTIFICATION OF SOURCES FOR FIGURES AND TABLES IN CHAPTER 2
BY NIPA TABLE AND LINE AND SMI CATEGORY

| LEGEND | SOURCE |
|---|---|
| Figure 2.1 | |
| International | Figure 2.2, Total |
| Domestic | Figure 2.8, Total |
| Financial | Figure 2.6, Total |
| General | Figure 2.7a, Total |
| | |
| Figure 2.2 | |
| Total | T316L7 + T316L11 + T312L18 |
| Defense | T316L11 + T312L18 |
| Other international | T316L7 |
| | |
| Figure 2.3 | |
| Defense purchases | T101L20 * T714L12/100 (1952–1971); |
| | T311L1 (1972–1993) |
| | |
| Figures 2.4a and 2.4b | Not from NIPA |
| | |
| Figure 2.5 | |
| Economic assistance | T316L9 (adjusted in 1991 to exclude financial |
| | contributions by other nations to the United States |
| | during Operations Desert Shield and Desert Storm) |
| Foreign affairs | T316L8 |
| | |
| Figure 2.6 | |
| Interest paid | T316L81 + T314L7 + T317L45 |
| Net interest paid | T316L81 + T317L45 + T314L18 |
| Interest (and dividends) received | − T314L7 − T314L18 |
| | |
| Figure 2.7a | |
| Total | T316L2 + T316L28 + T316L29 + T316L33 |
| | + T316L34 + T317L2 +T317L18 |
| | − T306L12 − T306L21 |
| Central activities | T316L2 + T317L2 |
| Net retirement | T316L28 + T316L29 + T316L33 + |
| | T316L34 + T317L18 − T306L12 − T306L21 |
| | |
| Figure 2.7b | |
| Gross retirement | T316L28 + T316L29 + T316L33 |
| | + T316L34 + T317L18 |
| Employer contributions | − T306L12 − T306L21 |
| Net retirement | T316L28 + T316L29 + T316L33 |
| | + T316L34 + T317L18 − T306L12 − T306L21 |
| | |
| Figure 2.8 | |
| Total | Sum of three lines categories below |
| Basic | T316L20 + T316L48 + T317L9 |
| | + T316L24 + T316L42 + T316L43 + T316L50 |
| | + T317L14 + T317L20 + T316L67 + T317L34 |
| | + T316L16 + T317L5 |

| Support | T316L27 + T316L30 + T316L32 + |
| | T316L35 + T316L44* + T316L45* + T316L47 |
| | + T316L49 + T316L51 + T317L21* + T317L22 |
| | + T312L23 + T312L24 + T312L25 + T312L26 |
| | + T312L36 + T312L37 + T312L40 + T316L10 |
| | + T316L53 + T316L54 + T316L56 + T316L58 |
| | + T316L60 + T316L61 + T316L66 + T316L74 |
| | + T317L24 + T317L28 + T317L32 + T317L33 |
| | + T317L39 + T312L39 + T316L37 + T316L78 |
| | + T317L40 + T312L15 + T312L17 + T312L27 |
| | + T312L32 + T312L33 |
| | *residuals after reconciliation with Table 312 |
| Other | T316L55 + T316L59 + T316L73 |
| | + T316L82+ T317L25 + T317L26 + T317L27 |
| | + T317L30 + T317L31 + T317L41 + T317L46* |
| | *includes roundings after reconciliation with Table 312 |

Figure 2.9
| Education | Figure 2.10, Total |
| Health | Figure 2.12, Total |
| Transportation | Figure 2.13, Total |
| Civilian safety | Figure 2.14, Total |

Figure 2.10
| Total | T316L20 + T316L48 + T317L9 |
| K-12 | T316L21 + T317L10 |
| Higher | T316L22 + T317L11 |
| Other | T316L23 + T317L12 + T317L13 |
| Veterans | T316L48 |

Figure 2.11       Not from NIPA

Figure 2.12
| Total | T316L24 + T316L42 + T316L43 |
| | + T316L50 + T317L14 + T31720 |
| Medicare | T316L42 |
| S/L medical care | T316L43 + T317L20 |
| Health and hospitals | T316L24 + T317L14 |
| Veterans | T316L50 |

Figure 2.13
| Total | T316L67 + T317L34 |
| Highways | T316L68 + T317L35 |
| Railroad and transit | T316L71 + T316L72 + T317L38 |
| Water | T316L69 + T317L36 |
| Air | T316L70 + T317L37 |

Figure 2.14
| Total | T316L16 + T317L5 |
| Police | T316L17 + T317L6 |
| Correction | T316L19 + T317L8 |
| Fire | T316L18 + T317L7 |

Figure 2.15
| Support: Individuals | Figure 2.16, Total |
| Support: Economy | Figure 2.19, Total |
| Support: Labor force | Figure 2.20, Total |

Figure 2.16
Total
T316L27 + T316L30 + T316L32
+ T316L35 + T316L44* + T316L45* + T316L47
+ T316L49 + T316L51 + T317L21* + T317L22
+ T312L23 + T312L24 + T312L25 + T312L26
+ T312L36 + T312L37 + T312L40
*residuals after reconciliation with Table 312

Social Security
T316L27 + T316L32

Welfare and social services
T316L44* + T316L45* + T317L21*
+ T312L23 + T312L24 + T312L26 + T312L36
+ T312L40
*residuals after reconciliation with Table 312

Veterans
T316L47 + T316L49 + T316L51 + T317L22

Supplemental Security Income
T312L25 + T312L37

Railroad Retirement
T316L30 + T316L35

Figure 2.17
Not from NIPA

Figure 2.18
Total
T316L44* + T316L45* + T317L21*
+ T312L23 + T312L24 + T312L26 + T312L36 + T312L40
*residuals after reconciliation with Table 312

Other
T316L44* + T316L45* + T317L21*
+ T312L24 + T312L26 + T312L40
*residuals after reconciliation with Table 312

AFDC
T312L36

Food stamps
T312L23

Figure 2.19
Total
T316L10 + T316L53 + T316L54
+ T316L56 + T316L58 + T316L60 + T316L61
+ T316L66 + T316L74 + T317L24 + T317L28
+ T317L32 + T317L33 + T317L39 + T312L39

Economic development, housing
T316L53 + T316L54 + T316L56 + T316L74 + T317L24
+ T317L28 + T317L39

Agriculture, natural resources and energy
T316L58 + T316L60 + T316L61 + T316L66 + T317L32
+ T317L33 + T312L39

Space
T316L10

Figure 2.20
Total
T316L37 + T316L78 + T317L40 +T312L15
+ T312L17 + T312L27 + T312L32 + T312L33

Unemployment Insurance
T316L37

Workers' Compensation
T312L17 + T312L32 + T312L33

Training and labor services
T316L78 + T317L40

Earned Income Credit
T312L27

Figure 2.21
Unallocable
T316L82 + T317L46*
*includes roundings after reconciliation with Table 312

Utilities and commercial activities
T316L55 + T316L59 + T316L73 + T317L25
+ T317L26 + T317L27 + T317L30
+ T317L31 + T317L41

Table C.2

IDENTIFICATION OF SOURCES FOR FIGURES AND TABLES IN CHAPTER 3
BY NIPA TABLE AND LINE AND SMI CATEGORY

| LEGEND | SOURCE |
|---|---|
| **Figure 3.1a** | |
| Total | T302L14 – T302L21 – T306L12 + T303L13 – T306L21 |
| Federal (public) | T302L14 – T302L21 – T306L12 |
| State and local | T303L13 – T306L21 |
| **Figure 3.1b** | |
| Total | T302L14 – T306L12 |
| Federal (public) | T302L14 – T302L21 – T306L12 |
| Federal Grants | T302L21 |
| **Figure 3.2** | |
| Total | T302L14 – T302L21 – T306L12 + T303L13 – T306L21 |
| Purchases | T302L15 + T303L14 |
| Transfer Payments | T302L18 + T303L17 |
| Net Interest | T302L22 + T303L18 – T303L21 |
| Subsidies less SGE | T302L27 + T303L22 |
| **Figure 3.3** | |
| Total | T302L14 – T302L21 – T306L12 + T303L13 + T306L21 |
| Regular | T302L14 – T302L21 – T314L8 + T314L7 + T303L13 – T314L19 + T314L18 + SMI(Total) |
| Social insurance | T314L8 – T314L7 + T314L19 – T314L18 – SMI(Total) |
| Employer contributions | – T306L12 – T306L21 |
| **Figure 3.4a** | |
| Total | T302L14 – T302L21 + T303L13 – T314L8 + T314L7 – T314L19 + T314L18 + SMI(Total) |
| Federal (public) | T302L14 – T302L21 – T314L8 + T314L7 + SMI(Total) |
| State and local | T303L13 – T314L19 + T314L18 |
| **Figure 3.4b** | |
| Total | T302L14 – T314L8 + T314L7 + SMI(Total) |
| Federal (public) | T302L14 – T302L21 – T314L8 + T314L7 + SMI(Total) |
| Federal grants | T302L21 |
| **Figure 3.5** | |
| Total | T314L8 – T314L7 + T314L19 – T314L18 – SMI(Total) |
| Federal | T314L8 – T314L7 – SMI(Total) |
| State and local | T314L19 – T314L18 |
| **Figure 3.6** | |
| Total | T302L14 – T306L12 |
| Regular | T302L14 – T314L8 + T314L7 + SMI(Total) |
| Social insurance | T314L8 – T314L7 – SMI(Total) |
| Employer contributions | – T306T12 |
| **Figure 3.7a** | |
| Defense purchases | T302L16 |
| Transfer payments | T302L18 – T314L10 + SMI(Transfers) |
| Nondefense purchases | T302L17 – T314L9 + SMI(Purchases) |
| Subsidies less SGE | T302L27 |
| **Figure 3.7b** | |
| Net interest | T302L22 + T314L7 + SMI(Interest) |

Grants                              T302L21

Figure 3.8
Total                               T302L14 – T314L8 + T314L7 + SMI(Total)
Program expenditures                T302L14 – T314L8 – T302L22 + SMI(Transfers)
                                    + SMI (Purchases)
Net interest                        T302L22 + T314L7 + SMI(Interest)

Figure 3.9a
Total                               T314L8 – T314L7 – SMI(Total)
Transfer payments                   T314L10 – SMI(Transfers)
Purchases                           T314L9 – SMI(Purchases)
Net interest                        – T314L7 – SMI(Interest)

Figure 3.9b
Total                               T312L3 – SMI(Total)
Social Security and hospital        T312L4 + T312L5 – SMI(Total)
Federal employee retirement         T312L11
Unemployment                        T312L6
Other                               T312L14 + T312L15 + T312L16 + T312L17

Figure 3.10
Total                               T303L13 – T306L21
Purchases                           T303L14
Transfer payments                   T303L17
Net interest                        T303L18 – T303L21
Subsidies less SGE                  T303L22
Employer contributions              – T306L21

Figure 3.11a
Total                               T303L13 – T314L19 + T314L18
Purchases                           T303L14 – T314L20
Transfer payments                   T303L17 – T314L21
Net interest                        T303L18 – T303L21 + T314L18
Subsidies less SGE                  T303L22

Figure 3.11b
Transfer payments                   T303L17 – T314L21
Net interest                        T303L18 – T303L21 + T314L18
Subsidies less SGE                  T303L22

Figure 3.12
Total                               T303L13 – T314L19 + T314L18
Difference                          T303L13 – T314L19 + T314L18 – T302L21
Federal grants                      T302L21

Figure 3.13
Transfer payments                   T314L21
Total                               T314L19 – T314L18
Purchases                           T314L20
Net interest                        – T314L18

Table C.3

SUPPLEMENTAL MEDICAL INSURANCE EXPENDITURES BY ECONOMIC
TYPE OF EXPENDITURE AND CALENDAR YEAR AS PERCENTAGES OF
GDP, 1967–1993

| Year | Total SMI (Total) | Transfers SMI (Transfers) | Purchases SMI (Purchases) | Net Interest Paid SMI (Interest) |
|---|---|---|---|---|
| 1967 | 0.15 | 0.13 | 0.02 | 0.00 |
| 1968 | 0.19 | 0.17 | 0.02 | 0.00 |
| 1969 | 0.21 | 0.19 | 0.02 | 0.00 |
| 1970 | 0.22 | 0.20 | 0.02 | 0.00 |
| 1971 | 0.22 | 0.20 | 0.02 | 0.00 |
| 1972 | 0.21 | 0.19 | 0.02 | 0.00 |
| 1973 | 0.22 | 0.20 | 0.02 | 0.00 |
| 1974 | 0.25 | 0.23 | 0.03 | −0.01 |
| 1975 | 0.29 | 0.27 | 0.03 | −0.01 |
| 1976 | 0.31 | 0.29 | 0.03 | −0.01 |
| 1977 | 0.32 | 0.31 | 0.02 | −0.01 |
| 1978 | 0.33 | 0.32 | 0.02 | −0.01 |
| 1979 | 0.35 | 0.35 | 0.02 | −0.02 |
| 1980 | 0.39 | 0.39 | 0.02 | −0.02 |
| 1981 | 0.45 | 0.43 | 0.03 | −0.01 |
| 1982 | 0.49 | 0.49 | 0.02 | −0.02 |
| 1983 | 0.53 | 0.53 | 0.02 | −0.02 |
| 1984 | 0.53 | 0.53 | 0.02 | −0.02 |
| 1985 | 0.55 | 0.56 | 0.02 | −0.03 |
| 1986 | 0.61 | 0.62 | 0.02 | −0.03 |
| 1987 | 0.68 | 0.68 | 0.02 | −0.02 |
| 1988 | 0.71 | 0.70 | 0.03 | −0.02 |
| 1989 | 0.73 | 0.72 | 0.03 | −0.02 |
| 1990 | 0.77 | 0.77 | 0.03 | −0.03 |
| 1991 | 0.82 | 0.83 | 0.02 | −0.03 |
| 1992 | 0.89 | 0.92 | 0.00 | −0.03 |
| 1993 | 0.91 | 0.94 | 0.00 | −0.03 |

NOTE: This table is derived from OMB (1993, 1995).

# REFERENCES

Ackley, Gardner (1961). *Macroeconomic Theory.* New York: The Macmillan Company.

Arrow, Kenneth J. (1969/1983). "The Organization of Economic Activity: Issues Pertinent to the Choice of Market versus Nonmarket Allocation," in *Collected Papers of Kenneth J. Arrow: Volume 2—General Equilibrium.* Cambridge, MA: The Belknap Press of Harvard University Press.

Auerbach, Alan J., Jagadeesh Gokhale, and Laurence J. Kotlikoff (1994). "Generational Accounting: A Meaningful Way to Evaluate Fiscal Policy," *The Journal of Economic Perspectives,* **8** (1), 72–94.

Bureau of Economic Analysis, U.S. Department of Commerce (1986). *The National Income and Product Accounts of the United States: Statistical Tables.* Washington: U.S. Government Printing Office.

Bureau of Economic Analysis, U.S. Department of Commerce (1988). *Government Transactions.* Methodology Paper Series MP-5. Washington: U.S. Government Printing Office.

Bureau of Economic Analysis, U.S. Department of Commerce (1992–1993). *National Income and Product Accounts of the United States: Volume 1, 1929–1958; Volume 2, 1959–1988.* Washington: U.S. Government Printing Office.

Chin, Audrey (1983). *Social Security—A Retrospective Look at Decisions for Complex Futures.* Santa Monica, CA: RAND, P-6876.

Comptroller, Office of the Secretary of Defense (1987). *National Defense Budget Estimates for FY1987.*

Dawes, Charles E. (1921). "Message of the Budget Director," in *The Budget of the United States Government for the Fiscal Year 1923.* Washington: U.S. Government Printing Office.

Derthick, Martha (1975). *Uncontrollable Spending in Social Services Grants.* Washington: The Brookings Institution.

Fisher, Franklin M., and Karl Shell (1972). *The Economic Theory of Price Indices.* New York: Academic Press.

Greenspan, Alan (1994). "Statement by Alan Greenspan, Chairman, Board of Governors of the Federal Reserve System, before the Commerce, Consumer, and Monetary Affairs Subcommittee of the Committee on Government Operations, U.S. House of Representatives, August 10, 1994," *Federal Reserve Bulletin,* **80** (10), 910–912.

Griliches, Zvi, ed. (1971). *Price Indices and Quality Change: Studies in New Methods of Measurement.* Cambridge, MA: Harvard University Press.

---

Korb, Lawrence J. (1993). "Growth and Decline of Accounts Through the Defense Investment Cycle," *Defense Analysis*, **9** (1), 89–96.

Kotlikoff, Laurence J., (1992). *Generational Accounting—Knowing Who Pays, and When, for What We Spend.* New York: The Free Press.

Langan, Patrick A. (1991). "America's Soaring Prison Population," *Science*, **251** (29 March), 1568–1573.

Lovell, Catherine H., and Charles Tobin (1981). "The Mandate Issue," *Public Administration Review*, **41** (3), 318–331.

May, Ernest R., ed. (1984). *Knowing One's Enemies: Intelligence Assessment Before the Two World Wars.* Princeton: Princeton University Press.

Mosher, Frederick C. (1954). *Program Budgeting: Theory and Practice.* New York: Public Administration Service.

Mussa, Michael (1994). "Monetary Policy: 1," in Martin Feldstein, ed., *American Economic Policy in the 1980s.* Chicago: University of Chicago Press for the National Bureau of Economic Research.

National Center for Education Statistics, U.S. Department of Education (1992). *Digest of Education Statistics.* Washington: U.S. Government Printing Office.

Newhouse, Joseph P. (1992). "Medical Care Costs: How Much Welfare Loss?" *The Journal of Economic Perspectives*, **6** (3), 3–21.

Office of Management and Budget, Executive Office of the President (1990). *Budget of the United States Government, Fiscal Year 1991.* Washington: U.S. Government Printing Office.

Office of Management and Budget, Executive Office of the President (1992). *Budget of the United States Government, Fiscal Year 1993.* Washington: U.S. Government Printing Office.

Office of Management and Budget, Executive Office of the President (1993). *Budget Baselines, Historical Data, and Alternatives for the Future.* Washington: U.S. Government Printing Office.

Office of Management and Budget, Executive Office of the President (1994a). *Budget of the United States Government, Analytical Perspectives, Fiscal Year 1995.* Washington: U.S. Government Printing Office.

Office of Management and Budget, Executive Office of the President (1994b). *Budget of the United States Government, Historical Tables, Fiscal Year 1995.* Washington: U.S. Government Printing Office.

Powell, Fred Wilbur, ed. (1939). *Control of Federal Expenditures—A Documentary History, 1775–1894.* Washington: The Brookings Institution.

President's Commission on Budgetary Concepts (1967). *Report of the President's Commission on Budgetary Concepts.* Washington: U.S. Government Printing Office.

Shryock, Henry S., Jacob S. Siegel, and Associates (1973). *The Methods and Materials of Demography.* 2nd printing (revised). Washington: U.S. Government Printing Office.

Smith, Harold D. (1946). *The Management of Your Government.* New York: McGraw-Hill Book Company, Inc.

Social Security Administration, U.S. Department of Health and Human Services (1990). *Social Security Bulletin: Annual Statistical Supplement.* Washington: U.S. Government Printing Office.

Stein, Herbert (1988). *Presidential Economics: The Making of Economic Policy from Roosevelt to Reagan and Beyond.* 2nd ed. (revised). Washington: American Enterprise Institute for Public Policy Research.

Volcker, Paul A. (1994). "Monetary Policy: 2," in Martin Feldstein, ed., *American Economic Policy in the 1980s.* Chicago: University of Chicago Press for the National Bureau of Economic Research.

Wark, Wesley K. (1985). *The Ultimate Enemy: British Intelligence and Nazi Germany, 1933–1939.* Ithaca, NY: Cornell University Press.

Weisbrod, Burton A. (1991). "The Health Care Quadrilemma: An Essay on Technological Change, Insurance, Quality of Care, and Cost Containment," *Journal of Economic Literature,* **29,** 523–552.

Wolf, Charles, Jr. (1988). *Markets or Governments: Choosing Between Imperfect Alternatives.* Cambridge, MA: The MIT Press.